Bridges, Beds, and other Important Things

By

Fredda J. Burton

Also By Fredda J. Burton

BOOKS

The Chocolate Set: A Swedish Journey
Ellis Island to the Last Best West
War and Storm
Way Too Many Goodbyes
Fleeting As Sunset
Only the Destination Was Wrong: Hanson-Persson Family History

Numerous Articles and Illustrations In
Mother Earth News
Countryside Magazine
Tidepools
Outdoor Illinois Magazine
Various Scientific Books and Journals
[Such as:
Forest Trees of Illinois
American Fern Journal
Illinois and Regional Plant Guides
Flora of Illinois]

Copyright Fredda J. Burton 2017

Dedication

To **ALL** of my HOME TOWNS

South Dakota: Spearfish, Lead, Deadwood, Belle Fourche
Washington State: Pasco, Pullman, Grayland, Port Angeles
Canada: Edmonton, Alberta, Vancouver, British Columbia
California: San Francisco, Los Angeles
Hungary: Budapest, Szeged
Italy: Florence
China: Hefei
Spain: Madrid

Introduction

This is my second book of 'One Minute' stories inspired by the ancient Chinese art of the very short story. The stories move from past to present in a somewhat orderly parade. A parade of words fashioned to represent part of a larger reality. I present them to you for learning and enjoyment. And a bigger goal: to entice you to write your own stories.

Writing does not have to be tangles of characters and plots and settings. Writing can be the formulation of your life and the stories you carry with you. You have been living stories from the moment of your birth. Dig out a pen and a pad of paper, or fire up that computer and get cracking. Your stories need to be told.

And while you are telling your own stories, the tales told by family members, friends, and the dim past will also appear. Use them, write them, make your own book! Thirty minutes a day will yield a living, breathing book by the end of a year.

Go now. Well, read my book first if you don't mind.

Long Ago and Far Away

Strong Drink

Great, Great, Grandfather Trond, was born on a mountain farm in the Valdres region of Norway. It was and is a land of steep mountains and rushing water. Small plots of arable ground dotted the lower regions and supported a small population of humans and livestock.

The self sufficient farmers made everything they needed from shoes to strong drink. Mostly Trond remembered making the alcoholic brew called *branvin*. Trond and his brothers took turns stirring the thick mash. His shoulders would ache and the pungent, earthy vapors from the brewing pan watered his eyes. Sweat aggravated a growing itch where his belt rubbed and his toes would grow numb from the cold. The glowing coals in the brew shed fire pit had little effect on the rest of the room. The stone floor was frost covered and ice formed on the rough hewn roof timbers.

He would beg his father to be allowed to stop, but no, the brew must be perfect. When he complained that it was such a lot of work for a little drink, his father would explain that it was more than drink, it was good fortune for the whole year.

Trond would grip the stirring pole and attack the malt and water mixture with new vigor.

They had soaked barley in water for three days to make the malt. When the wet grain began sprouting, it had been spread to dry. The next day the dried malt was ground in the farm mill. The dry malt was then mixed with warm water in the brewing pot, a pot that served as the family wash pot the rest of the year.

When Trond thought he could stir no more, a great ruckus erupted outside. Three boys burst into the room. Old custom dictated that the ale be brewed with a show of strength and vigor. The roaring fire beneath the brew pot was often accompanied by wrestling matches among the young men of the family. Lifting one another to the ceiling and grip contests added to the atmosphere. When Trond was relieved of his stint of stirring, he tackled his younger brother, Erik, and pushed his face into a puddle of spilled mash. A bigger, brasher neighbor boy grabbed Trond by the hair and hauled him across the room.

He shook free of his tormenter just as Erik slammed into him from behind. All three of the boys lost their footing on the crusty floor and fell in a heap.

They asked if they could sweep the mess out the door.

"Ah, boys. The dirtier the floor, the better the ale."

"Pappa and his old sayings," muttered Erik. He wiped the drying mash from his face. "Better we grind the barley into flour and make honey cakes."

An hour and a session of arm wrestling later, Pappa Kjorstad announced it was time to let the mash rest. They covered the brew pan and dragged the *rostekar* from its place behind the door. The large stave vessel looked like a barrel, but it had an open bottom. They lifted the *rostekar* into place over a regular barrel with a sieve between. It had been lined with straw, yarrow, and juniper sprigs with their gray berries intact. The boys hoisted the brew pot and poured the steaming mash into the *rostekar*. It would slowly strain through the mat of twigs into lower barrel.

The resins in the juniper would add a certain strength and flavor to the ale; the yarrow increased the inebriant quality of the brew.

~~~

Two weddings, a baptism, and a house warming later, Trond found himself encouraging his father to increase the amount of yarrow in the brew. After his first heady cup he had been hooked.

The freedom he felt drove him to dance and flirt with abandon. Why had he been denied this experience so long. Certain that the fair Anne across the valley reciprocated his feelings, he planned his every journey outside his home place so he passed by her door stoop. Life was good in the Valdres Valley of Norway.

    In the late 1860's Trond and Anne emigrated to America where they acquired a large farm in the Dakotas. At the turn of the century Trond died in a farm accident and left a legacy of twelve children, most with a tendency toward alcoholism. Old custom had morphed into modern disease.

4

The Great Wolf Hunt

The Dakota Farmers' Leader, Canton, South Dakota's newspaper, announced the wolf hunt on Friday, January 12, 1900:
"Will Chase Them Down

**Blood Thirsty Hunters Will Trail the
Ferocious Wolves to
Their Lairs Jan. 16**

The sports of Beloit and Canton have decided to look for wolf scalps next Tuesday, and we give the words of the poster which announces the coming event:

A grand wolf hunt is being arranged for Jan. 16, in a territory about ten miles square, Canton being on the north line and Forest Hill cemetery on the west line. Everybody is invited to join in the hunt and be on that part of the line nearest their residence at 9 o'clock in the morning of Jan. 16. The start will be made at ten o'clock. No guns will be allowed and all dogs must be kept chained until the word to loose them is passed along the line by the various captains. Those joining the hunt are expected to go on foot except the captains who may be mounted. The round up will be on the Keep farm east of the river."

Sixteen year old Charlie read the Friday paper with new interest. The hunt seemed a real break from January's monotony. Though the weather had been unusually calm and snow free, school work and everyday chores had done little to fill his time.

"Just be careful," advised his mother. "Your cousin, Tom, will be here for a few days. The two of you can go hunt wolves together."

On Monday Charlie noted in his diary that Cousin Tom had arrived. "To-morrow we expect to have a great time hunting wolves. Cloudy looks like snow." In the meantime Tom paid a visit to Grand Valley school where Charlie was a senior, then helped him with his after school chores.

After an afternoon of pitching hay, shelling out corn, and cleaning one of the cow sheds the boys tucked into a supper of potatoes and gravy, roast beef, and home canned green beans. By the time they got to the apple pie exhaustion was setting in. "Too much competition to see who could work hardest the fastest," said Charlie's father. "You should visit more often, Tom."

On Tuesday morning Charlie wrote: "This is the day of the great wolf hunt. We are up early for chores and breakfast. I will take my wheel [His bicycle. Charlie did not like horses.] to the starting point. Tom will ride the brown mare."

As the two boys headed for the dirt road that marked the western boundary of the hunt, they were joined by several dozen neighbors and visitors. At the starting point they found a number of wagons and buckboards and a temporary hitching rack for the riding horses. The hunt was to be on foot.

While Tom tethered the brown mare, Charlie found the captain of this section of the hunt to ask for instructions. The two boys were assigned the section nearest the river, perhaps because it was the most difficult terrain and the boys were strong and eager.

Right on the dot, at 10 o'clock, a volley of gun shots set the hunt in motion. The boys scrambled through the rocks and dry brush to their position on the bluff. They had been instructed to turn any critters trying to double back to freedom.

From their high perch they could see the lines of people moving across the landscape. More hunters descended from the Sioux Falls train stopped on the prairie.

"Look at that," said Tom. "There must be a couple hundred people from the city."

"Those varminty wolves don't stand a chance."

By noon the lines of hunters had reached the Keep Farm, Tom and Charlie among them. At first the crowd was cheerful with jovial questions about the wolf count, but as the word spread an aura of dejection descended over the hunters. The crowd dispersed to make the long walk back to the tethered horses and lines of buggies.

The next day the newspaper and Charlie's diary reported "No wolfs captured. Only one jackrabbit. Over 500 people present."

I expect the wolves were sitting on their haunches on some far away bluff laughing their heads off. The jackrabbit was released on his own recognizance.

8

The Ice Cream Wagon

On June 4th of 1907 my grandparents married in Sioux Falls, South Dakota. By the following June they were settled in a sod house in Perkins County on the other side of the state. After the birth of three children and the acquisition of a car they moved to town.

After several job changes that included county clerk, general store proprietor, and sheriff, Charlie Hanson opened a meat market complete with a cooling room and a freezer.

His next bright idea was to get a bit more use from the distinction of having the only cold storage facility in the county—ice cream. He cleared out a corner of the store, built a counter and installed stools and two small tables, much like a bar. Voila! A soda fountain.

Of course his wife, Hilma, was saddled with the task of mixing up the milk, eggs, sugar, and flavorings for the ice cream. Her tiny, ill equipped kitchen and several very young children under foot made the task more difficult. She mixed up small batches at a time and poured them into a tin milk can. The can held 10 gallons so this was an afternoon's work.

When she had the milk can full, she walked and dragged it outside to a small wagon. It was the job of the two oldest children, Lester and Ardis, to pull and push the wagon to the market.

This perilous journey was always scheduled for early Saturday morning so the finished product would be ready for sale in the evening when the ice cream parlor did most of its business.

If you think loading and hauling that milk can of ice cream to the parlor was an easy task, try again. A ten gallon can filled with milk weighs about 80 pounds. The street was rutted dirt with an uphill stretch and a fair amount of traffic. The kids were ten and twelve years old and paid only with a sample of the finished product.

One overcast weekend the kids complained about making the delivery. They were told that Pappa was waiting for them and a little rain never hurt anyone.

By the time they had pulled the wagon to the sloped part of the road it was pelting hard and they were screaming at each other to go faster. The wheels of the wagon had picked up so much mud that they could barely turn.

Straining to get a little momentum for the hill, Ardis tripped and lost her grip on the handle. The wagon lurched backwards, knocked Lester sideways, then toppled into the ditch. Unfortunately the lid of the milk can popped off and the ice cream mix oozed out on the ground.

The can they delivered to the meat market-soda fountain was less than a third full. Punishment was quick and severe. No treats for a month, no outings with playmates, and extra chores. They were lucky to have gotten by without a whipping.

Much to the embarrassment of the children the story of the ill fated ice cream was told over and over through the years.

Of course no one remembered the many weeks when the children successfully brought the wagon with its sought after ice cream mix to the store. Only the spilled mess was mentioned. Again and again.

The Birthday Book

When my brother, Chas, moved from West Seattle to Honolulu, he sent me a box of family junk he had accumulated over the years. A few very old photos, newspaper clippings, receipts, and a small book. It probably didn't lighten his load much, but gave him a sense of relief to be unburdened.

I gave the book a quick look, then tossed it in a drawer. It was about the size of a pocket New Testament. Its light green cover and thicker sewn in pages indicated it was something else. The first printed entry read: *'1 Januar. Benrif Bieregaard 1792 Unfer fabt'* or something like that in old Gothic script.

Directly under this in pencil was written: Martha Steensland 1887. The next printed entry read: *'2 Januar. Prof. G.B. Odersberg 1783.'* And in pencil and with elegant flourishes was written: Emil Hanson 1885. My grandfather's brother.

The green book was a birthday book with a place for each day of the year, the name of someone famous that shared the birthday, and a short poem or quotation on the facing page. A gold mine for anyone searching for family history. Still, it was several years before I looked at it again.

Birthday books were very popular around 1900-1920. Many were in Danish, but this one appeared to be in old Norwegian or Swedish. To complicate the job for the reader or translator, the printed portions of the book were written in tiny ornate Gothic script.

On line translation was no help. One site was convinced the language was Welch, another thought it was German. Wrong. And neither offered up a meaning in English.

Thumbing through the book, I recognized the names of friends and neighbors of the Hanson family back in Canton, South

Dakota. Names like Torberson and Steensland flooded the pages along with several generations of Hansons. Mostly folks born in the 1860's, 70's, and 80's. Those born later were mainly people from the Western side of the state in Perkins County.

Along with the shift in age and location came a decided change in the handwriting. The ornate flourishes became the plainer, often cramped writing of a people with much work to do and little time for the pretties of handwriting. Still, they took the time to sign the birthday book.

By now I was convinced the book belonged to my grandfather, Charlie Hanson. He was born in the Canton area, went to school there, then moved West to homestead in the Bison area. In June of 1907 he married Hilma Peterson and the following June they moved to a sod house on the prairie of Perkins County.

When I reached the month of April, I found my grandfather's name. The printed entry read: *'9 April Henriette Gislejen. 1809.'* The penciled entry under that note said *'Chas. Hanson 1881 Canton, S. D.'*

The lady, Henriette, who shared that birthday remains a mystery like the others in the book. A poet, a doctor, the publisher's old auntie. Who knows? On line searches of people born in 1809 have come up totally empty as have the names for all the other days of the year. The poems and quotations on the facing pages were more forthcoming. Kant, Goethe, Grimm, Ibsen, and more obscure writers marched through the year.

My grandmother, Hilma, had immigrated from Sweden in 1903. She had had a fairly thorough education in her homeland and learned to speak English quickly. The written word was harder, but she was making great headway until she met up with her future husband, Charlie. Even the birthday book bore evidence of his stubborn, domineering attitude.

In the space for birthdays on the 26th of June, Charlie had penciled in her name in as 'Mrs. Chas Hanson 1886.' This crabbed entry was crossed out with explosive ink strokes and re-written in her elegant script as 'Helma Peterson 1885.' All her future life with Charlie was summed up with this entry. He continued to insist she had been born in 1886 and that he knew her name was 'Hilma.'

She continued to retaliate by crossing out the offensive name and date whenever she could. Eventually she gave up on the spelling of her name, but then refused to acknowledge that she knew how to write English.

We unearthed another example of this feud in an old trunk in a cousin's attic a few years later. It was Charles and Hilma's wedding certificate. Well, it was half of the marriage certificate. The top section with the names of the couple had been ripped off so that only names of witnesses and other information remained. Could be that Hilma shredded the offending part of the paper with her name and birth date. Maybe, hopefully, she cooked it into her husband's oatmeal one morning.

Many times over the years Charlie probably regretted his stubborn actions when he could have used her help in his various business endeavors. And there is probably an old saying to cover this. Hopefully I'll remember it soon. 'Cutting off your nose to spite your face,' maybe.

14

Bison to Spearfish 1926

My grandmother, Hilma, seemed to have little use for embroidered table cloths, knick-knacks, fancy clothing, picture books, and the general detritus of life. She could have packed her possessions into a couple of apple boxes. She was always giving away things she had accumulated.

Her husband, Charlie, on the other hand, was a genuine pack rat. Cheese boxes, cigar boxes, apple boxes, barrels all filled to the brim with buttons, nails, washers, rocks, bits of greasy metal. Stuff was stacked to the ceiling of the shed out back.

Hilma had banished her husband's junk from the house long ago, but the piles of stuff continued to grow. They rose to the ceiling in the shed, blocked the windows, and made it difficult to open the door. Barrels of car parts, wagon parts, old horse shoes, moldy books added to the mess. Only it really wasn't a mess in the sense that it was an unorganized pile.

Charlie had spent hours organizing and labeling his collection. The cheese boxes became small elongated drawers with hand written notes detailing their contents. Bent nails in one box, straight nails separated according to size, washers in another box, bolts and nuts kept separate from ordinary screws. Sometimes he taped an example of the box content to its front.

He must have had four or five trailer loads of stuff in that shed and that presented a dilemma when the family decided to move the 135 miles to Spearfish. The older children urged him to haul it all to the dump: Hilma thought he should just close the shed door and walk away. He refused to do either.

While Hilma packed up the household goods, Charlie collected parts to build a trailer. It turned out to be a fairly respectable vehicle, but Charlie had underestimated the sheer weight of his junk. Halfway through the loading, the left side tire-wheel assembly collapsed and spilled things everywhere. Hilma stormed out of the house and took one look at the mess, then flapped her apron at the rising dust and retreated into the house. Charlie, not one to react much, threw his hat on the ground and stomped it into oblivion.

When the Hansons moved south later that month, the pile of junk and the broken trailer sat near the shed as a monument to their leaving. Years and years later a bunch of us grandchildren paid a visit to Bison. We asked around if anyone knew the location of the old Hanson house. 'Can't miss it,' said one of the old timers. 'Just look for the white house with the rusty wheel and axel in the front yard out near the highway.'

Babe White and Devils Tower

In August or September of 1926 my grandfather, Charlie Hanson, moved his family south from Bison, South Dakota to Spearfish. A wife, four teenagers, two pre-teens, and baby Carol. They found a house and settled in, as much as they usually did and just in time for school in the fall.

The Hansons had packed up and moved from Canton, South Dakota to a sod house on the prairie to several different houses in the small community of Coal Springs, then to Bison where Charlie built a tiny house, then a bigger one, and then moved to an existing house where baby Carol was born. That made at least seven moves in sixteen years.

Charlie had changed jobs and professions as many times as he moved in those years. Sodbuster, farmer, store owner, ice cream parlor operator, Clerk of Courts, sheriff, carpenter. It was this last occupation that prompted him to move his family south. Bison had a population of 310 while Spearfish was a metropolis of 1,930 people.

While his wife, Hilma, scurried to make the new rented house comfortable, the children stepped up to make friends and figure out new schools. By the time the unpacking was accomplished Charlie was hip deep in the real estate business. Selling houses was far easier than building them.

New Year's Day of 1927 was a Sunday. The Hanson family spent New Year's Eve at a party at the Methodist Church. It was 60 degrees. The next day the family joined the church. Monday it was back to work talking real estate and driving potential buyers around the county looking at houses, barns, cabins, empty tracts of land. The weather turned nasty and the New York Stock

Exchange sold stocks at an all time high. The first trans-Atlantic phone call was made.

In February there was an incident with Hilma and a pair of bootleggers, but that's another story. Mostly she cooked and cleaned and kept the kids in line. Spearfish had many pitfalls and temptations not found on the desolate prairie of their previous home.

The oldest daughter graduated from high school in 1927, the Hansons moved to a bigger house, Charlie sold acres of real estate and caught more fish than he had ever seen before. And, of course, brought them home for Hilma to clean and cook. She also used a hundred pounds of sugar in her canning and baking, kept up with church functions, and family picnics.

Her efforts netted her the aggravation of her varicose veins and a blood clot. Charlie drove her the fifty some miles to the hospital in Rapid City on August 17 where she remained until September 8th. The rest of the family headed home. They did manage to return for several visits in the twenty-two days she was there.

A couple of weeks after her discharge from the hospital the whole family drove to Rapid City for Hilma's follow up appointment. While they were in Rapid, they watched Babe White, the Human Fly scale the Harney Hotel, one of the tallest buildings in the city. Perhaps it was to make it up to Hilma. She had missed Babe White's climb of Devils Tower over the state line in Wyoming while she recuperated at home.

It was the last recorded climb of Devils Tower using the wooden stakes called The Ladder. The stakes had been driven into a series of cracks in the formation's lower surface in 1893. They would get the climber to the area called 'The Lawn.' After the lawn it was fewer stakes and greater dependence on ropes and cables.

On September 11, 1927 the 'Human Fly' had climbed the Tower. Despite the difficulties of getting there, it was a huge event with some 500 or more attendees. That was some sort of record considering the mud roads into the area, the lack of a bridge over the Belle Fourche River, and the lack of facilities at the site. Many people came on horseback.

The Hanson clan minus Hilma and baby Carol arrived on the scene a little before noon. Not wanting to get stuck in the mess of cars, wagons, and people, they parked near the turn off and hiked the rest of the way in. The boys lugged the picnic lunch and the girls ran ahead to find a good spot. Babe White was already on his way up the vertical rock.

Shortly after the Hansons finished their lunch, the Human Fly made it to the top of the 'ladder,' dropped his climbing gear, and waved vigorously to the crowd. 350 feet down, 900 more to go.

To the sound of cheers, gun shots, and blaring horns he gathered up his ropes, crossed the 'lawn,' and started up the taller part of the rock. Near dusk he reached the flat top of Devils Tower. He again turned to the patient crowd below. This time he did a little dance, pulled a small flag from his coveralls, and waved before beginning his descent.

By anchoring one end of his cable to the rock, shimmying down, releasing the upper end of the cable and re-attaching it, over and over, he made quick work of getting off the rock. The gathered crowd was much slower. A terrific traffic jam developed and Charlie gloated all the way home over his smart move to park at the main road.

Babe White was last climber to use the ladder in his climb. The lower 100 feet of the concoction of stakes and 1'X4's was removed to discourage climbers. Today a bridge spans the Belle Fourche River and the roads are paved. Several hundred climbers make the trip up Devils Tower using modern climbing techniques each year.

20

Famous Folks

Charles Lindbergh Lands In Spearfish

While Charles A. Lindbergh was landing in Paris on May 21, 1927, the first non-stop flight across the Atlantic, Charlie Hanson wrote in his diary that he had sold the Powers house to Roy Simmons for $1800, watched the graduation of his oldest daughter, and read about an earthquake in China that killed 200,000 people.

When Lindbergh returned to the States, he took a victory lap around the country, 82 cities in 48 states. One of his stops was Spearfish, South Dakota.

On Friday, September 2 at 11am The Spirit of St. Louis landed at the grass air strip just east of town. Nearly everyone in town waited for the tiny plane to wheel to a stop and a huge cheer went up. This was big time entertainment. Charlie wondered how Hilma would react to his taking the morning off while she was cooped up in the hospital in Rapid City. No matter. This was important stuff.

The mayor stepped forward with a gilt cardboard key to the city; state government people elbowed their way to the front to shake hands; a small child made a presentation of a floral bouquet, then ran back to mommy sobbing. Col. Lindbergh requested water, then pulled off his helmet and doused his head. A very short speech, a towel, and a toilet break completed his visit. He climbed into the refueled plane and taxied to the end of the short runway and lifted off.

Charlie was already magnifying his non-role in the proceedings into a good story as he walked back to his car.

Encounter with the President, Coolidge That Is

Family legend has it that one of the Hanson clan had a close encounter with a United States president. Real, imagined, or just a close call—it is hard to tell after all these years.

The president was Calvin Coolidge and the year was 1927. In his attempt to escape the heat, the bugs, the press, and the continual harassment by the political community of Washington D.C., Coolidge accepted an invitation to visit the calm and quiet of the Black Hills in Western South Dakota. He stayed most of the summer.

Calvin Coolidge and his wife, Grace, arrived in Rapid City at 5:30 pm on June 15. My grandfather, Charlie Hanson, noted in his diary that it was a Wednesday. On June 19 the presidential couple attended church in Hermosa, a small town near the Game Lodge. Such was the beginning of the new summer White House.

The couple did not hole up and keep to themselves, rather they attended events throughout the area. They were underfoot at every rodeo, parade, fair, livestock show, and celebration in Western South Dakota. They seemed to be alone and it was not uncommon to find oneself elbow to elbow with Coolidge at an event. Apparently the Secret Service contingent assigned to the president was small and very, very bored with looking at cattle and cowboys.

One weekend Coolidge added another activity to his repertoire—watching buffalo and feeding the wild donkeys that roamed the Game Lodge. The Hansons with their three boys, seventeen year old Lester, fifteen year old Clarence, and seven year old Millie were parked along the narrow blacktop road enticing a group of long eared beasts with sugar cubes when a long black car pulled up and stopped in the middle of the road.

The hubbub caused by the presidential car and the large mess of gawkers following it frightened off the animals for a few minutes, but the vision of sugar cubes soon brought them back. The Coolidge party elbowed its way to the front, but Lester refused to give up his position as head donkey feeder.

A photographer tried to push the teenager aside to allow Coolidge a photo op with the wild animal. Lester and the donkey held their ground for a few seconds before a flash bulb went off. Up went the donkey's head, then he whirled around, kicked back, and galloped off through the brush.

Coolidge lost his balance and stumbled into Lester. He stepped on the teen's newly polished shoes and knocked his hat off before the secret service agents hauled the him back to the presidential limo.

Lester picked up his hat, dusted it off and said, "Well, darn. Presidents are more dangerous than wild animals." And the story of being stepped on by a president entered our family history.

My Good Old Days

Cooking Lessons at the Roundup Cabins

The year my father finally came home from the mess and bother of the 1940's we set to work becoming a proper family. That proved to be harder than we thought. My dad had a job in Belle Fourche as watch maker at Seth Smith's Jewelry store. My mother worked as a nurse at John Burn's Memorial Hospital. Us kids were nearly ready to start school. We needed to find a place to live in Belle Fourche.

Belle was a cow town of about 3000 people. Most of them had lived there their entire lives in houses inhabited by their parents and grandparents. Other than a garage or shed no new construction had occurred since the 1930's.

I figured out that I had moved more than a dozen times by the time I reached my fifth birthday, lived in three states, four towns, and more houses than I could remember. 'Home' was a pretty meaningless word.

We asked everyone we knew as well as a host of strangers about a possible place to buy or rent. We drove every street in town looking for a vacant place. Of course there was no such thing as a real estate agent. Finally someone suggested the tourist camps and motels. The two motels in town said 'no' to long term tenants because they were booked up most of the year because of various events. That left one possibility.

The Roundup Cabin Camp. It was a circle of small cabins wedged between the railroad tracks and a curve in the highway near the high school. The 'cabins' were abandoned grain storage buildings that once dotted the prairie to the north of town. A few windows were cut in each one and a floor built to divide the tall structure into two one-room spaces. A narrow stair connected the two floors and a tiny bathroom was built under it.

My folks signed a nine month lease and went to Grandma's house in Spearfish to get our trailer. Back at our new home we unloaded bedding and household stuff, but left most of our junk in the trailer parked next to the cabin. We had made yet another fresh start on our life journey.

One really cool thing emerged from our stay at the Roundup Cabin Camp. My brother and I had our first cooking lessons. The cabin's simple kitchen was comprised of a narrow counter along one wall with a tiny fridge under one corner and an old gas stove.

For that first lesson my mom pulled up two of the kitchen chairs to the counter for us to stand on, then seated herself on the nearby couch. Detailed instructions for us very small kids followed. Wash your hands. Find the blue mixing bowl and the big spoon. Sugar and flour and such—no mixes for us. Measuring cup, chocolate chips—oh, we were making chocolate chip cookies.

We measured and mixed until our efforts passed inspection, then she demonstrated spooning the dough onto the cookie sheet and turning on the oven. My brother and I finished loading the dough onto the cookie sheet. I think the neighborhood dog could have done it better, but we were praised like crazy.

We stood back while she popped the cookies into the hot oven and were told we were excused from cleaning up the mess—this time. The finished product looked pretty wacked out, but tasted just fine. More praise flowed our way.

Ahead of the next lesson we were shown the recipe on the chip package and told to copy it out on a sheet of paper. A big chore for kids who had yet to enter the first grade, but we managed.

By the third week we had to double the recipe and put the cookies in the oven ourselves. We needed a bit of help on that one. Another week we made brownies from a mix. That was when we were also expected to clean up our mess.

Other meal fixing chores joined the cookie making over the months we spent in that cabin. Soup—ah, that was an easy one. Tear up the remains of the roast and toss it in the pot with potatoes and carrots peeled and sliced by Mom. No knives yet. Bread, yes we actually made bread. Yeast was a fascinating thing.

Jell-O, red and orange with a can of fruit cocktail, was a real chore with all that stirring. We ate a lot of the stuff with funny grainy spots in it because of our inadequate stirring, but no one complained.

We were never strictly bound by recipes other than as lessons in arithmetic and probably developed a feel for proportions as a result. Praise was always far more important than precision.

When our stay at the Roundup Cabins ended because our lease was up, we found a rackety old house to buy. Moving superseded cooking for awhile. Once we got settled, our cooking sessions moved to Sundays when we spent the day prowling the forests of the Black Hills. We would get up early to cook up a pot of stew or chili or make Swedish pasties for our lunch out on some deserted trail or the ruins of an old mining town. My brother and I had a major part in that cooking.

Later, after we moved to Washington State and I entered the eighth grade, cooking supper became an after school activity several days a week. The preparations were much more complex by this time. And we could use knives which meant peeling things, finally. My mom would sit in the living room writing and only answered my questions about oven temperature or timing a roast beef with short, shouted comments.

My brother had his turn on alternate nights. By this time he was much more interested in complex recipes he found in exotic cook books. Before long his cooking out shown my simplistic approach to eating by miles. In either case, those long ago cooking sessions in the Round Up Cabins served us both well. Every child should be so blessed.

Chicken Pox and the Boiler Room Nurse

Back in the 1950's chicken pox was just another hurdle of growing up. No shots, no parties with an infected kid to get the bug at a convenient time. Just a for sure part of a kid's life.

We got the bug in the winter of 1952. After a few days of misery and a lot of scratching my mom paid off the baby sitter and sent us back to school.

I presented my excuse, an short note written on the back of a used envelope, to the teacher who initialed it and sent me to the office. After dodging the big kids on their way to home room on the second floor I gave my note to the principal's helper. She told me to take a seat and disappeared into the next room.

After a ten minute wait she returned and handed me a paper with my note attached. Take this to the nurse, she said.
Glad to be out of the office, I hurried downstairs, out the back door and across the playground to the high school building where the nurse's office was located. In the basement.

Fortunately I didn't have to dodge the big kids because they were in class by then.

The nurse sat behind a desk piled high with folders and books. To hide her detective novel and box of chocolate covered cherries I figured. The room was otherwise empty.

She took my paper and ordered me to a chair across the small room. I sat down with my book bag at my feet and waited. And waited. At first the extreme heat in the room felt good, but soon enough I started looking for its source. The wall behind me felt hot to my palm and I soon realized the nurse's office was just an extension of the boiler room. The heating system for the entire school was just inches away.

Though she had no other students to attend, the nurse made me sit in that pool of sweat for over a half hour. She examined the spots on my face, asked me how long I had been out of school, then told me to call my mom.

Can't, I said. She's at work.

I went back to my seat by the boiler and listened while she called our number without success. Next she called the hospital where my mom worked as a real nurse. They said they would relay the message. I was in for some big time sweating.

When the phone finally rang, I tried not to listen to the hot words between the school nurse and my irate mother. It was not pretty.

The whole business filled the morning and I finally slipped out of the boiler room and walked to the front steps where I knew my dad would show up to take me home at lunch time.

The next morning my mom wrote me another excuse and dropped me off at school. Once more I ended up in the sweat inducing nurse's office. Once more she denied me entrance to class and I spent the rest of the morning sitting on the school steps. It hadn't helped that my mom had accused the school nurse of being under educated and only qualified to empty bed pans.

This feud had no winners, but I was a clear loser. A whole week of school spent between the boiler room heat and the snowy front steps. The following Monday my scabby, itching skin had healed and the school nurse reluctantly signed my excuse allowing me back in class.

An Odd Bridge

An odd bridge dominated my years in Western South Dakota. It crossed the Belle Fourche River in the middle of town. It was the only link to the highway north and the route through Montana to the west. We lived on the north side of the river and had to cross it to go to work, school, and the Safeway store. In the summer dozens of threshing crews with all their equipment traveled north over the bridge. The Bentonite plant hauled its product south across the bridge to the railroad. It was one busy place.

The bridge was a sturdy affair with a steel girder top that was painted yearly, a pedestrian walkway, and a black topped deck. Unfortunately, the bridge wasn't straight. It had a corner right at the south edge of its super structure. The clearance on a straight approach was barely enough to allow the thrashing machines and heavily loaded trucks to clear. On the corner it was impossible.

When an over height vehicle came to the corner it stopped, completely blocking the bridge. The driver would get out and hiss enough air out of the tires to let his vehicle pass. Then, on the other side, he had to air them up again. Sometimes by hand, sometimes with a compressor. A very slow and tedious business.

The threshers traveled in groups so this was an all day blockage of the bridge. A few drivers had tried to get across the bridge by unloading, but that method was quickly abandoned. Easy enough to get the cumbersome machine off the truck, a tricky bit of work to get it back aboard. As the wheat crop in the north ripened we knew we were doomed to walk to town via a rickety suspension foot bridge about a quarter mile downstream.

     This glitch in the bridge probably had a fair part in Belle Fourche's lack of growth over the years. The problem remained when we packed up and moved to Pasco, Washington. It wasn't until a visit we made back to the old home place some dozen years later that we realized the old bridge had been replaced with a straight, topless structure. Traffic could wiz through town and on to northern destinations with barely a second look at Belle

     A new visitor center sprawled in the space vacated by the old bridge approach. Standing on the overlook I couldn't help but remember past incidents that played out there.

The Bridge Game

No, this is not a story about a card game. It is about a real life bridge connecting one side of a river to the other side. School kids living on the north side of the Belle Fourche River had two choices for their trip from home to school and back. One was the highway bridge, the other a creaking, swaying suspension foot bridge closer to the school.

You modern folks will think this whole idea of walking to school very primitive. We had no school buses, no lunch program, and probably other 'no's I haven't thought of yet. When a student reached the end of the sidewalk at the street, the school's responsibility ended too. You were on your own.

In the winter when the snow was deep most of us chose to take the highway bridge home. It did have a pedestrian walkway so mingling with the steady flow of truck traffic was an optional plan. Most of us stuck to the walkway where the main danger was the blowback of snow, slush, and general crap from the traffic.

A few of the sixth grade boys had other ideas though. One big kid had perfected the art of grabbing onto the right rear of a truck just at the place where the license plates attached to hitch a free ride across the bridge and on up the hill. Some days he would hike back down and have a second trip.

That sort of amusement became less than fun the day he made a mistake and ended up under the wheels of the truck. Two broken legs kept him out of school for the rest of the year.

Another near fatal mishap happened because we were stupid enough to enjoy jumping off the bridge rail into the huge snow banks on the flood plain below. Nice pillow-like snow usually gave us a soft landing, but one day my buddy, Ronnie, jumped too close to the bank and impaled himself on a metal fence post. That proved to be far worse than getting run over by an empty cattle truck.

Someone ran to the nearby Elks Club to call for help. The police chief sent us all racing for home, so we never saw the blood and gore of getting Ronnie off the fence post. He was hauled off to the Belle hospital, but then moved to a big city hospital in the eastern part of the state. He survived, but we never saw him again.

That was the last time I ever walked across the big bridge over the Belle Fourche river.

The Foot bridge

When we moved to Belle Fourche in 1947, the only house we could find was on the north side of the river. That meant that everything was across the river from us. Banks, shops, school, and hospital. On our side we only got credit for a filling station and the Methodist church, the road to the city dump, the Bentonite plant, and the sales barn. Not very helpful when the bridge was closed. The next bridge was a hundred miles away in Wyoming.

Some years before we arrived on the scene, the city had decided to build a foot bridge across the Belle Fourche River to make it easier for the north side kids to get to school. A suspension bridge was constructed from the main street at the post office, across the river, and through the flood plain on the opposite side to a point about six blocks from our house.

The plank floored bridge was much maligned and much used. One would have thought half the school children in town lived on the north side by the foot traffic on the bridge at 3:30 in the afternoon. Most of them didn't. The high school kids came for the recreation of tossing rocks and bottles into the murky water and swaying the bridge. Most would cross, then turn around and head home.

My first encounter with the foot bridge was about halfway through the first grade. My mom called the school to report she had a double shift at the hospital and couldn't pick me up after school. The teacher relayed the message and asked me if I wanted to make a phone call to someone else. I shook my head 'no.' The very idea of making a phone call was too daunting. I had never even touched a phone in my whole life. I would walk home.

My walk to the bridge was easy enough. A couple of gangs of big kids passed me, but paid me no attention. The bridge was another matter. By then the oldest Streeter boy had caught up with me. He was also a first grader, but tougher and much more independent. We walked together in silence. He was the son of Mexican seasonal workers who had decided to winter in Belle. I wasn't even sure that Carlos could speak English.

There was a large group of high school kids on the bridge when we got there. The wooden bridge planks seemed uneasy, loose and slippery. But since no one else was afraid, I started across. The water seemed far, far down and very fast and swirly.

I walked closer to Carlos. He didn't seem to mind. By the time we reached the middle of the bridge it was swaying wildly. The gang of big boys had succeeded in getting the bridge to buck along its center rather than side to side. Kids were bouncing off the railing and running for the bank until we were the only ones left on the bridge.

That's when things got ugly. One big boy called Carlos a wetback and other bad things. He had to scream to be heard over the racket of the bridge. The others joined in the taunting. They got so wrapped up in their insults, they forgot to rock the bridge for a minute. Carlos and I joined hands and ran for home just as fast as we could.

The next day I told my teacher what had happened. For the rest of the school year that gang of boys had to stay after school long enough to give the little kids a head start.

Portable! My Eye

I was much surprised when the tape, CD, radio combination I had ordered arrived in a huge box. This thing was supposed to be portable. Maybe they just used an oversized box to accommodate all the packing material.

No such luck. When I hauled the player from its wrappings, it was humongous. Barely fit the shipping box. The only feature that qualified this monster as portable was the sturdy handle on top. I could have cried, but I didn't. Too much trouble.

It reminded me of another, far more wrenching disappointment of long ago. A Christmas disaster for my brother and me.

When the Christmas catalog arrived that fall, we spent hours making out the perfect wish list. We had been promised at least one gift of our choice to make up for the skimpy holidays of the past few years.

Not daring to ask for fancy presents like bikes, we finally settled on a set of walkie-talkies we thought would add a nice touch to the many scenarios we acted out with our friends on weekends and vacations. Little handheld receivers powered by batteries.

We presented our short list in early December and waited with baited breath. This could be a fun year. We even hinted to our buddies about the expected gift.

Christmas morning finally arrived. And like my tape/CD player, the box seemed way too big. We hauled the present from behind the tree to the middle of the living room. We poked and prodded the bright wrappings, then tore into it.

The flimsy interior box said it contained a toy field telephone set. Big and heavy the central phone and two receivers soon lay on the floor demanding four double D batteries each.

Twelve batteries, not included. And even without the batteries the field phones, each the size of a large book, were not portable.

We barely heard my dad exclaiming about the realism of the phones and we'll have this baby up and running in no time.

Close to tears, we went back to unwrapping new shirts and socks, a postcard album from a great aunt in South Dakota, and candy from a neighbor.

When Mom called us to breakfast, my brother stood up and gave the field phone a kick before heading to the kitchen. Engrossed in reading the instruction sheet for the phones, I don't know if my dad even noticed.

Popsicle delivery

A woman who lived down the street from us worked at the local dairy and bottling company. The place made an array of juices, soft drinks, and frozen treats along with the more traditional milk things. Their specialty was popsicles. Probably born of the need to use up the tail ends of the other things they produced.

All during summer vacation we listened for the popping backfire of her junky car. Every Friday and Saturday around 3 o'clock we would hear her as she crossed the bridge over the Belle Fourche river to the north side.

Our gang of six would be waiting by the picket fence along the road past our house. She would roar up the gravel road and slide to a stop amid our cheers. Her son was one of our younger gang members.

She would get out and open her trunk while we waited to see the day's treat. She had an old cooler that held a collection from the week's cast off frozen treats. Popsicles with one stick, lopsided ice cream bars, flavors and colors mingled in impossibly ugly shapes and sizes.

One of the worst combinations was the end of the grape flavored popsicle run mixed with leftover lemon crème bar. We called those ugly treats pukesicles. Fudge bar mixed with cherry fizz looked pretty awful too, but tasted just great.

In any case we enjoyed those odd ball treats produced by a factory unwilling to clean their equipment between flavors. For several summers we snarked down freebies enough to spoil a good many suppers.

But all good things usually come to an end. The state health inspector put an end to our orgies. 'Flush and clean your system before the next product,' they ordered. This also curbed the great variety of flavors produced for sale. Too much labor and down time for the machinery. The dairy went back to the standard fare of ice cream bars, fudge bars, and two flavors of popsicle. A great loss in my opinion.

Sherry and the Cherry Red Lipstick

Way back in 7th grade I baby sat the little girl next door most week days after school. While her mother went to work as a waitress and her father slept in preparation for his night shift, we roamed the neighborhood. It was usually an orgy of messing around, into everything, affair.

Sherry was a real firecracker. She had friends all over the four square blocks where we lived and some days it seemed like we saw them all. In and out of kitchens, laying in the dirt shooting marbles, wrestling with dogs, dressing squirming cats in doll clothes. Mud pies, water fights, rock throwing. Paying me to babysit was a bit like hiring the fox to guard the hen house.

That all changed the day I showed up at her door to find her in a dress with her hair done up in curls.

Instead of shrieking and running down the street to terrorize the pug with the bulging eyes next door, she took my hand and we walked sedately across the driveway to my house. She greeted my mom politely and sat down at the table for milk and cookies. I asked Sherry if she was feeling sick, but she shook her head no.

Our afternoon romps had suddenly turned into one prolonged tea party. Sometimes we tip-toed back into her house where Sherry tried on all the dresses in her closet. And shoes. And hair clips and ribbons. I was pretty flabbergasted. Not only by my charge's change of attitude, but also by her humongous wardrobe. I had one dress for Sunday school and special occasions. And one pair of shiny patent leather dress shoes. Sherry had dozens.

Who knew. And how could a bartender and a waitress afford all this stuff for their kid anyway.

Things escalated the day Sherry found a lipstick somewhere. Maybe at an aunt's house or in some nook or cranny of her mom's stuff. I had never seen her mother wearing makeup of any kind, but who knows what lurks in someone's drawers or old purses. Sherry was hooked.

Her vaguely pink lips grew redder and redder as she got bolder. My mom would have forbidden it and snatched the lipstick away. Sherry's mom just watched and waited. Or maybe she was too tired to notice.

By the time of Sherry's birthday party, the red lips had entered the realm of the absurd. I was invited and in spite of being the giant among a gang of babies, the promise of unlimited cake and ice cream was too good to turn down. And rumor had it that sometimes the guests would receive presents as well give them.

Sherry's red lips were front and center, especially in the photos snapped by her dad. Big and bright, they outshined her blond curls and new dress. No queen in the midst of her court could have out shown our girl that day, but it was pretty much the last gasp of red lips.

The next week rumors of a government warning about the red coloring agent in all foods and cosmetics filtered across the Dakota plains to our small town. Bing, bang, no more red lips. The tea party was over. No more finger curls and frilly dresses. We went back to throwing rocks and sloshing through mud puddles. Who would believe that laying in the grass and kicking our bare feet could be such a relief.

Fire at the Ford Garage
Or One Hot Car

I was in the first grade in Belle Fourche, South Dakota at the old Washington School. The big sandstone block building sat near the river and almost on my mom's route home from her job at the hospital. When her schedule meshed with school dismissal time, she would wait for me at the street and we would walk home together.

Our route took us past the post office where we always stopped to check our box, then we crossed the suspension bridge to the north side where we lived. Some days we walked an extra couple of blocks to pay a visit to my dad at his job at Seth Smith's Jewelry Store down on Main Street. Our route to downtown passed by the bakery and the Ford garage.

One day we were waiting to cross the street near the garage when a huge fire ball shot out of the double doors to the service area of the garage. Lucky for us we were still across the street because that thing barreled past us and ended up in a clump of lilac bushes on someone's lawn. The sound of the explosion followed and the dry bushes burst into flames.

Now some folks would say we should have high tailed it out of there, but we didn't. We stood on the curb and watched the mechanics push a burning car out of the garage to the street. By the time we closed our mouths the city fire truck pulled up with half its volunteer fire fighters.

The first round of water seemed to make the flames squirt higher and splattered them everywhere. Gasoline and motor oil no doubt. Someone got smart and rustled up a few bags of sand

and poured it on the worst of the flames. It was all over except for the cleanup. We continued our walk home.

The Tale of the Teeny, Tiny Sewing Machine

My brother, Les, e-mailed to say he was sending over a package of 'stuff' he had neglected to bring on his last trip to the Peninsula. He included the tracking number and insurance information, but no hint at what he was sending.

A day early a very small box appeared in my mailbox. The mailing label was bigger than the box and wrapped around it. Whatever he had sent, it was miniature. And it was—a plastic sewing machine made way back in the late 1940's or early '50's by Renwal. 'No. 89' was molded on the back along with 'Made in the U.S.A.'

Looking at the detailed little doll house accoutrement did little to jog my memory. When the lid was opened, the machine could be folded out like the real thing. It had a wheel on the right that moved a tiny needle up and down. And the two drawers could be pulled out. Only the treadle was missing.

The miniature machine must have been a part of the doll house someone gave me for Christmas back before I started school. I had wanted a play ranch complete with fences, trees, cattle, horses, and a tin bunk house, but received the urban house instead. It had no horses, so it was soon relegated to the closet.

My brother wasn't even on anyone's radar at that time, so my mom must have preserved the doll house or at least the sewing machine through many moves. Several years later I did get my play ranch, but all that remained of that was a rubber bull and a spotted cow. Even the horses I had added later had vanished.

I placed the sewing machine on the shelf in my office and went back to writing these stories. After a few days the blue toy with its yellow lid demanded more attention and I looked it up on the internet. I didn't find a blue sewing machine, but two yellow ones came up on E-Bay. Their treadles were intact.

Thinking I could scavenge the treadle from one of them for my machine, I placed a bid. Six days and $24.00 later my second toy sewing machine arrived in the mail. In a much larger box with wads of green foam packing material and yards and yards of tape. So much for environmentally friendly packing.

Detaching the treadle was easy. Installing it on my sewing machine not so much. It fit, but flopped around like a drunk kitten. There seemed to be several ways to install the thing because there were two holes and three pegs on each leg of the toy. Several more than the treadle required. I must have missed something. Back to the internet to look at other Renwal toy machines.

Sure enough—I had the treadle installed backwards. A quick reversal and it worked perfectly.

In my rush to restoration I had not once wondered why I had such a need to make my toy whole. And now I had a second one without a treadle. Did I have to buy another one to fix it? I suddenly envisioned a hundred toy sewing machines lining my desk, my end tables, the kitchen counters. An endless procession. Something was wrong with this picture.

About this time I got an e-mail from the lady who had sold me the yellow toy. Apparently my feedback had not extolled her virtues sufficiently. Her house was full to overflowing and she was getting old. She really, really needed to find good homes for her massive doll collection. I reassured her that her toy sewing machine had found a good home. No need to explain that I had pillaged her treasure for parts.

I finally gave her now incomplete toy machine to a doll collecting friend who seemed to be less rabid about fixing things.

Third Grade Horrors: The Marble Jar

Third grade in Belle Fourche was held in an ancient brick building across the playground from the new second grade building. The low one story second grade school had been built specifically for small children with everything brand new and scaled to fit, Second grade had been fun. Not so for third graders.

The two story cube of a building with steep stairs and creaking floors was a real come down from the sleek kid friendly school we had attended the previous year. It seemed like it had been built for giants. And not very particular giants at that.

The water fountains required a box to stand on and nearly everyone just held it rather than try the antique toilets with their pull cords to flush. It was always a crap shoot to see if you would be rewarded with a spray of nasty water. Doors were almost impossible to open with their ancient push bars and warped frames. Even the surplus desks and chairs were tall and clunky and only the very biggest kids could touch their feet to the floor. The rumor hinted that the building had been used by the basketball team in years past. Or strong giraffes.

To top off the horrible building we had the worst of the worst teachers that year. She was a student teacher from a nearby college and had no love for us. She had hoped for a big city assignment for her student teaching and instead she got us cow town brats.

The first day of school she set a gallon jar on her desk, then proceeded to strip us of our marbles, knives, and keys. The marbles went in the jar. Forever, she said. Knives and keys were returned at the end of the school day. The only thing she permitted on our person was a handkerchief.

One of the things we dreaded most was fire drill. Our room was on the second floor near the stairs to the ground floor. The other classes took that route when the fire bell rang. Not so us. In the corner of our room a door opened onto a metal fire escape. We were required to exit the building that way. The steps were see through grating and the hand rail was so tall it was almost out of reach. In some places the bolts holding the whole affair to the brick wall had pulled out and the stairs barely clung to the wall.

Still, we made the climb down the side of the building regularly to stand on the edge of the playground until we were allowed back in the building. We did get to go back to our classroom by the main entrance.

Somehow we survived that school year, but it seemed like a total bust until the last day of school. We had expected some sort of party, or at least a reprieve from the usual routine that last day, but the marble jar sat on the teacher's desk and she was lining up the kids for the usual pocket search. Jack knives in a pile on one side, keys and toys on the other.

She almost gloated when she seized a shooter and a dozen cat-eyes from the kid in front of me. She dropped them into the nearly full jar and all hell broke loose. The jar cracked wide open and marbles spilled everywhere.

We were on the floor instantly, scrabbling through the broken glass in search of our long lost marbles. The mess quickly devolved into a free-for-all. Thirty five kids wallowing in the mess of upturned desks, books, papers, glass shards, and marbles punching each other. The teacher climbed up on her desk and set to screaming like a wounded banshee.

With our pockets bulging with marbles and wounds leaving smirches of blood on floor and desks and clothing we retreated to the back of the room.

Third graders may not know the meaning of words like absurdity, farce, and ludicrous, but we almost instantly and in chorus started laughing. We laughed so hard, we cried. We were still in hysterics when the principal burst into the room. She ushered the still screaming teacher out of the room to the office. At the door the principal turned to us, winked, grinned, and said she would send up the school nurse and the janitor. Also a box of candy bars.

    We never saw that teacher again. We all passed and found that fourth grade was actually fun.

Jell-O Eggs

Last Easter I happened to be in a large department store with a prominent display of tools, pans, gizmos and gadgets for the preparation of Easter dinner. At eye level sat egg molds for making gelatin Easter eggs. Along with the molds was a large card displaying generous instructions for making and decorating the eggs.

Back in the 1950's we made Jell-O eggs three times a year for Turkey Day, Christmas, and Easter dinners. Big time for Easter. Betty Crocker probably would have been horrified at our method. We used real egg shells for our molds.

In January we would start saving shells. My dad had made a pipe gizmo to blow the eggs out of their shells without punching a hole in their bottoms. Every time we wanted eggs for breakfast or for baking we would use the pipe thing to blow the egg from its shell. About one in ten resulted in a whole, useable shell.

We would rinse both the egg shell and the egg blower with salt water with the hope that this would rid us of grime and bacteria. That was probably wistful thinking, but no one ever got sick.

As Easter approached, our stash of empty egg shells grew. Cartons of them sat waiting on the top shelf of the cupboard. A few days before the big dinner we began mixing up batches of Jello-0. One of every color. We always urged our mom to skip yellow ones as we did not like the flavor. She ignored us and said the colors had to balance. An art lesson. Who knew.

Easter morning we had to peel the shell from the eggs and return them to the fridge as quick as possible. It was a messy job, but the one we liked best. We were cleaning up bits of egg shell for weeks after the holiday.

Presented on a plate lined with lettuce, the eggs always stole the show at mealtime. Some of them were dressed with a sprig of parsley, a slice of green olive, or a fancy spurt of salad dressing. The platters were empty by meal's end. No one ever thought to ask about the process we used to make them.

Friday Night Vigil

In August of 1955 we moved from the Midwest to Pasco, Washington. It was like moving to a different planet. For one thing we had TV for the very first time. Four channels of black and white bombardment invading our new house. Talk of war, accidents, death and destruction right alongside cartoons, Red Skelton's Comedy Hour, and various quiz shows. It was hard to know what to think.

Especially for us cow town isolationists. Our four page newspaper reported parades, rodeos, school plays, wheat and cattle prices, who was visiting from out of town, and sales at the Golden Rule store downtown. One of the first things my mother did after we moved was to subscribe to the old hometown newspaper. A bit of nostalgia to cling to.

The next thing she did was to investigate the local Ground Observer Corps. We had lived in the shadow of a major air base in South Dakota and felt its aura of protection for years. Now in this far West Coast location she felt undressed and vulnerable. Not too strange for folks who remember the years of turmoil caused by World War II.

The DEW Line or Distant Early Warning System was in its early phases of construction, but was still several years from readiness. The civilian Ground Observer Corps would have to do for the years between. My mom signed up and asked if I could too. They said sure though I was only thirteen. The more eyes the better.

About twenty of us met for a short orientation with maps, pictures and diagrams of various planes. A signup sheet with the unmanned hours of the local observation post marked in red was passed around. My mom signed us up for Friday from nine to midnight.

The observation post was on the roof of a grocery store four or five blocks from our home. Probably another one of the reasons we selected this new activity. The twelve by twelve structure had windows all around, a phone with a direct connection to headquarters in Spokane, office-type chairs, a sort of wide angle viewer aimed at the northern sky, and my favorite, a Big Ear listening device.

We rarely saw an aircraft we didn't recognize in the short span of daylight we had before dark and planes after dark were few and far between—maybe three a year. Activity on the ground was much more interesting.

I quickly discovered the Ear could be pointed in the direction of the street. When the movies let out, I could listen to the conversations of people below. Tired children out long past their bedtimes, boyfriends trying for one more free feel from a girl weary of fending off his groping hands, married couples thrashing out an old quarrel, would be movie critics extolling or deriding the movie. Topics were endless and far more interesting than nonexistent war planes flying the desert sky.

One night, not long after the movie crowd had dispersed, we heard sounds of a scuffle from the Big Ear. It was full dark and the circle of illumination from the street light showed nothing. The street appeared empty. The sounds escalated and became screams. Desperate, pleading screams.

We had no phone connection with anyone except the military tracking station near Spokane. We had never had occasion to call them so had no idea if we would connect with a real live person. What if we triggered something. Worse—what if we did nothing.

With trepidation, fear, and trembling we picked up the phone. A calm voice answered, listened, and assured us they would connect with local police immediately. We hung up and waited.

Within a few minutes the sound of sirens over powered the screams coming from the Ear. Red lights reflected in our windows and running footsteps came from both ends of the alley below. Slamming car doors and loud demanding voices poured from the Ear and rattled the windows. It was over in a minute, quicker than we could move to turn the Ear skyward. Only the faint sound of an approaching ambulance remained.

Whatever was going on in the streets below, we had done the right thing. A few months later we attended an affair where pins and awards were handed out to various members of the local Ground Observer Corps. Mostly membership pins and a bar for one year of service. I thought it was too bad they couldn't give one for work above and beyond to the Big Ear.

Jewel and the Big Horse Racing Day

My most recent uncle, Uncle John, joined the family via a late in life marriage to my mother's oldest sister. It was a second go around for both of them. They seemed to make the arrangement work, but the rest of us viewed their union with trepidation and at times, fear and loathing.

John was a back slapping, butt pinching, huggy-kissy, loud mouthed fellow. The exact opposite to my family of quiet, laid back Swedes.

There was one bright shining spot in this odd coupling and that was Uncle's John's sister, Jewel. She lived in Spokane, a city a hundred or so miles from us. Trying to cement family relations and curry favor, my Auntie invited me to go with her and Uncle John to the horse races at Playfair race track outside of Spokane.

It would mean putting up with Uncle's bad jokes and touchy feely ways for a whole day, but I gave in to my interest in horses and agreed to go with them. What none of us knew was that race tracks in Washington State had an age minimum of 16. They turned us away at the ticket window. Uncle John said he would talk to someone, but in the meantime we would pay a visit to Jewel who lived a few miles away. Maybe we could get into the track the next day.

She fed us and offered to put us up for the night. Uncle John and my Auntie opted for a hotel room leaving me and Jewel by ourselves. Since this was the first time I had ever spent more than a few minutes with her, I was nervous.

Not for long though. Jewel led me through her house to examine her treasures. Every nook and cranny held an antique bowl or vase or figurine. Each of them had a story. We sat on her rosewood settee until bedtime re-living the history of her life, drinking diet soda and munching our way through a huge bag of potato chips.

I slept like a rock and woke to the fairyland of Jewel's guest room. Brocade curtains, an old oil painting of a unicorn at the foot of the bed, an antique oriental carpet wall-to-wall, velvet robe and slippers, and a tray with a small pot of coffee and a huge cinnamon roll on the side table. Magic personified.

Later she said that she thought a few changes in my attire and a bit of makeup would get me past the gate at the race track. Forget about her brother's complaining to the track board of directors and all that nonsense. It had worked for her kids and grand kids. It did and Uncle John never did figure out a way to take credit. Two victories in one weekend.

Marty Robbins and the Stolen Car

Way back in the late 1950's a popular entertainment in the Tri-Cities was the concert-dances held at the civic center in Kennewick, Washington. A small dance floor, casual seating, and a snack bar coupled with dim lighting, small entrance fee, and a huge parking lot made this a well attended venue.

A few times a year live music replaced the DJ. One of those live performers was an up and coming country western star by the name of Marty Robbins. Big stuff for this sagebrush community.

I had a casual date for that show. He was a senior boy in my current events class. A cute boy. Ray said he would pick me up at eight. I dolled myself up, accepted the obligatory emergency phone call dime from my mother, and answered the honk from the car at the curb. A spiffy dark red Chevy with tan upholstery. He said it belonged to his old grandmother.

The line for the concert was forming up by the time we arrived, but it moved quickly. We entered the low building in time for the warm up band's first set. We found a table near the stage, but Ray complained that it was too bright so we moved to the back.

By the time Marty Robbins and his band took the stage Ray seemed jumpy. Somewhere in the middle of 'White Sport Coat and a Pink Carnation' he excused himself. At intermission he had not returned, but at the concession bar he suddenly appeared at my elbow.

He wanted to know if I could get home by myself.
What's wrong?

Don't ask. He gave me a quick hug and disappeared out the door.

I waited until the concert was nearly over before calling my mom from the phone booth in the lobby. She arrived just about the time the band finished their last set. She looked question marks at me, but said nothing.

A few days later Ray's picture stared out of the morning paper. Car theft, taking a stolen car across state lines, resisting arrest. The pristine Chevy belonged to a local businessman. He didn't think Ray was very cute.

The Boy in the Turret Room

Back in high school a small group of us fell into the habit of meeting at Jackson's house to play cards, tease, talk, and just hang out. Jackson lived with his grandfather in the old section of town we always called the East Side.

The neighborhood grew from the need for housing for the railroad workers at the nearby hump yard back in the early 1900's. One cluster of the old Victorian style buildings still remained in the midst of pre-fabs, surplus Navy homes, and old trailers. A gas station with a mini mart took up the highway side of the neighborhood.

Jackson lived in one of the two story Victorians with a turret room. The pretentious exterior of the house masked the total disarray of the interior. Piles of newspapers and magazines rose from floor to ceiling. Boxes and boxes of greasy car parts, old clothes, books and dishes filled every inch of space on the ground floor. Jackson's grandfather was a hoarder.

The second floor was bare except for the cot and dresser in Jackson's room. He was spared the extreme clutter because Grandfather was too old to climb the stairs.

Jackson was a couple of years behind us in school. He was a lousy student, but a crack card player. Watching him shuffle and deal a double deck of cards was like magic. He seemed to know the position of every card.

We spent many Saturday morning hours sitting on the floor of the turret room watching our allowance money pile up in front of Jackson. I think his dream was hopping a bus and heading for Los Vegas. But, who knows, Jackson wasn't much for talking.

What we did know was that there was little love lost between him and his grandfather.

When we walked up the path and waited to be ushered into the house, we could hear the yelling and cursing rocking the old building. It would be a sullen and sometimes bleeding Jackson who opened the door. We would troop up the stairs to the turret room trying not to notice the old man with the folded belt in his hand. The weapon reserved for Jackson's punishments.

As our junior year wore into spring, we spent less time in the turret room. By May we were engaged in a torrent of school activities. On top of that Jackson skipped school more and more often and was quickly becoming a distant memory. Until one rain drenched morning.

We were getting ready for school. My mom turned on the TV for the early weather report. Instead of the usual TV fare a grainy black and white news feed came on. Excited voices were reporting a police action on the east side. The dim pictures showed a half dozen patrol cars and an ambulance in the street. A house with a turret loomed in the background. Jackson's house.

School was forgotten as we watched and listened to reports of gunfire, a wounded police officer, and the possibility of one dead inside. The shooter was holed up in the turret room. While the TV camera panned the scene, a team of policemen charged across the lawn with a ram in an attempt to batter in the front door. The face we saw pressed up against the turret window was Jackson's.

The highway patrol with sirens screaming joined the local police about the time the battering ram bounced off the front door. Seems that old carved door was the strongest part of the house. Jackson took advantage of the diversion to send a spray of bullets into the cars, then he smashed out the remains of the window and tossed his weapon out.

We heard later that they found him sitting on the floor shuffling his double deck and humming to himself. His grandfather and a policeman were dead, another patrolman was in the hospital. Except for the newspaper report the next day, we never heard from or about Jackson again. Too young to be charged as an adult, he simply disappeared into the juvenile system. Maybe he eventually found his way to Los Vegas or maybe he occupies a cell at the State Penitentiary. A real waste all around.

Another Waste, Another Bridge

I had a last name friend in high school. Three years of next to next existence. What is a last name friend anyway? The school was a stickler for lining us up alphabetically according our last names. Johnny and I were both 'A's.' in a class of 'M's,' 'L's,' and 'S's.' We were together at the head of every line.

We sat next to each other in every assembly, pep rally, rehearsal, and presentation. We sang together, held hands, pledged this and that, and marched around the gym and up and down the aisles of the auditorium. We stood together in endless lines, waited patiently for speakers and buses—all in the name of keeping order.

What we didn't do was ever see each other outside of school or talk about family, dreams, and future plans. We lined up one last time in June of 1960 for graduation. I doubt if either of us ever thought of the other again.

Except, when years later, I was forced to remember Johnny. It was 1979. I was back in Pasco to visit family when the headlines of the Tri City Herald screamed out at me one morning. *"Woman Drops Kids Off Bridge."*

Rumors and speculation started flying back and forth amongst old classmates because the woman was my last name friend, Johnny's wife or ex. Some said she had been ordered to return the two young boys to their father and chose to murder them instead. Others thought she belonged to some weird cult that believed the only way to save children of divorce from hell was to kill them and send them on their way to heaven before it was too late. Some believed it was drugs or drink that had prompted her. Total insanity was another possibility.

No matter the reason, the children were dead. The bridge was high, the Columbia River swift and deep and filled with ice chunks. It was February and the two and three year old boys were dressed in heavy coats, hats, scarves and mittens. The newspaper article detailed the mother's story of how she parked on the bridge and carried the boys one after the other and dropped them over the railing. It was months before their bodies were recovered.

While classmates speculated, I worried and wondered about Johnny. How did such a straight arrow of a guy meet up with this depraved woman? He was a successful engineer and building designer, she was a high school dropout waitressing in a truck stop.

And how do I erase such vivid horror from my mind? How do I get the memory of Johnny back to the sweet guy from high school assembly? And worst of all—how does Johnny keep on keeping on?

Wedding, Pretty Much

In the summer of 1961 my future husband told me it was now or never. I was enrolled in summer school at Columbia Basin College in Pasco, Washington with a couple of super boring classes like Shakespeare and mid-century poetry. Future husband had finished his teaching year at the college and gone back to the university. A long dreary drive through sagebrush and wheat fields separated the two locations.

A wedding. Good grief. The thought had never entered my mind. But, why not? It was easier to go with the flow than argue the matter. We set the date for early August, changed it a couple of times, then settled on the 5th. Pasco was in the midst of one of its worst heat waves in history. I would be finished with summer school, and future husband was getting impatient.

We got the Unitarian preacher out of bed and scheduled the ceremony. Neither of us had ever seen him before, nor had we ever crossed the threshold of his church. It seemed like neutral ground. We wrote up a handful of invitations and mailed them to an odd collection of people—mostly a few relatives and friends. Some of them agreed to be part of the wedding. We were collectively short of such things.

At the JC Penny store I found a white party dress on sale for twelve bucks. A trip to the dime store turned up a headband with plastic flowers, also white. I borrowed my mother's white sandals a size too big and bing, bang, I was all decked out for a wedding.

I ordered a cake at the grocery store, my dad bought a case of beer. Someone else rummaged around and found a suitable table cloth. My old Junior high homeroom teacher volunteered her daughter to sing at the ceremony.

The night before we got drunk as skunks, at least I did. Next morning was one big hangover. Auntie gave me a blue pill which nearly sent me to la, la land. The preacher was late because he forgot and was vacationing at the beach. We were a scraggly bunch when we gathered in that stifling hot church to shuffle through the ceremony.

But we did shuffle through. My hangover lifted, I got out of that itchy sale dress and too big shoes, we ate the cake and drank the beer, and climbed into a borrowed Oldsmobile and headed down the Columbia River to Honeymoon at the ocean. And lived happily ever after.

My Scrape the Bottom of the Barrel Wedding Or Another Take on My Wedding Story

While watching one of the 'judge' shows on TV decide on damages in a case of a ruined wedding gown by a dry cleaner, I realized the world had passed me by—the wedding world anyway. Even with inflation an eight thousand dollar wedding dress seemed absurd. If the dress cost that much, how about all the other expenses?

I always thought the weddings of several of my relatives were overly extravagant, but they never reached this level. And then there was my own wedding.

In the short vacation time between summer quarter and fall term at Washington State University my intended and I decided to tie the knot. And that's pretty much what we did.

We approached the pastor of the Unitarian Church in a nearby town and asked if he would perform the ceremony the first week of August. He said 'Sure, but you have to clean the church first. We don't have services in the summer.' Maybe God was on vacation then.

I inked up some invitations and mailed them. Postage and envelopes added up to $10.00. I ordered a cake at the supermarket for $8.00. 'Be sure you pick it up the day before.' 'A dress,' my Auntie said. 'You need a dress.'

I stopped by Penny's and found a sale rack of unsold prom dresses. Lucky for me one of them was white and it almost fit. $12.36 including tax. I made a veil from a headband, a lace hanky, and a strip of fake flowers from the dime store. Cost: $1.39. Shoes were a bigger problem. All I had were tennies and black oxfords. My mother said I could borrow her white sandals. 'A size too big, but you're not going on a hike. Slow down and they won't flop much.'

'Flowers' someone said. I told my future husband, then dismissed the idea. He showed up at the church with a gob of red roses. He also ordered a keg of beer. Beer and marble cake with lavender frosting in my parents' back yard for the reception.

We did, in fact get married, though I don't remember much of it. The preacher forgot and went on vacation. We had to roust him out to drive back for the ceremony. He made a strange speech and sent us on our way. We gave him a meager $15. Less than his gas money.

Total cost: about 46 cents a year so far. Some sort of a bargain.

I wore the white dress a couple more times. Mostly to parties with a red sash to disguise it's wedding connotations. Then I dumped it in the thrift shop donation box. The dime store veil or what is left of it is in my junk drawer. So much for weddings. My cheap one out lasted my cousins' pricy ones by about fifty-four years.

The Musket in the Moving Van

When the movers unloaded our motley belongings at our rented house in Edmonton, Alberta, things looked okay. After three years at Washington State University our stuff was mainly books and papers with a few odds and ends of household items and clothes. The mover had squeezed our boxes in with a load of more conventional items like tables, chairs, beds, and cabinets of a professor going the same way.

When we got to unpacking our boxes, a fine cloud of orange dust puffed out of some of the boxes. Closer examination revealed small puncture wounds in many of our boxes. When we got to the kitchen stuff, we realized the orange dust was really curry powder, turmeric, and cinnamon. The spice cans were punctured through and through. It was all very odd, but not much of a loss.

Until I got to the box with my knick knacks that is. My Ming horse in his nest of foam and crumpled newspaper was in pieces. I had bought the porcelain beast from a roadside vendor the summer we spent in Downy, California. A whole $7.98 down the drain. His hollow body revealed several small lead pellets. Shot. Who the heck was shooting in or at a moving van?

The moving people apologized, then told us they would investigate. Turns out the guilty party was a loaded pistol, an antique muzzle loader belonging to the professor. It was probably the best possible place for the thing to shoot off its load. No one was hurt. I dumped the remains of my Ming horse in the trash and forgot the whole thing. Until now, sixty years later.

Whether the pistol was impounded at the border, they didn't say. No guns were allowed into Alberta without special permit, especially loaded ones.

72

Countdown in Huston 1967

Early in 1967 we flew from Southern Illinois to Huston, Texas for a math meeting. While my husband sat through dozens of boring talks on obscure math topics, I tried to find something interesting in the big city.

Shopping was a bust and one more lunch at an 'Irish' pub would have broken the boredom bank. I finally decided to visit the city's brand new Astrodome. A little investigation showed that it was a straight shot from the hotel to the stadium via the city bus. Fifty cents would get me a morning's entertainment.

A bus ride can illustrate the size of a city and that was really the case with Huston. It was a good many miles from the city center to the end of the line in the Astrodome parking lot. Eight miles and seventeen minutes to be exact. The Dome was open for visitors, so I had a good climb up a batch of steps to view the interior. Big. Empty. Okay.

Back in the parking lot I noticed a lot of commotion in a nearby building. Big cars parked out front. Suits with bulging pockets and crossed arms standing guard at the doors. I walked past them without comment.

Inside, a boxing ring nearly filled the small room. I was eyeball to kneecap with two sweaty boxers. I had to back up into a doorway to see the goings on. And it was going on. A sparring session between the newly re-named Cassius Clay and a nameless sleek muscled unknown.

Mohammed Ali circled and punched, rippled and dipped across the ring. His speed and grace made his opponent look like a well rooted oak tree. Ten minutes later the trainer dinged the bell and tossed Ali a towel.

A nearby poster announced the coming title fight in the Astrodome. On February 6th Mohammed Ali would fight Ernie Terrell. The heavy weight title of the world was on the line. There was history being made here at the end of Huston's bus line. Who knew?

When Ali climbed through the ropes and jumped down, a helper held his robe for him, then began pushing a path through the crowd. He was rough and a bit full of himself.

When they got to me, the helper moved to push me aside. Ali stopped him and gave me a quick bow, grinned and brushed my cheek with his sweaty glove. Greatness takes many forms.

Old Main Burning

    Saturday night June 7, 1969 we were having a casual party in the gray split level house we rented in Tatum Heights, Carbondale. A couple dozen staff and students from Southern Illinois University sat around our living room drinking beer. A lot of beer.
    The conversation was summer school and vacations, pets and children. The mix of math people and art people, strangers to each other, carefully avoided talking about the anti war demonstrations in the Student Center in previous months, the bombing of the Agriculture Building in May of 1968, the attempt to burn down or blow up the Chemistry Department by leaving some fifty gas jets open in a lab, the tent city occupied by undergrad art students on the lawn of Allen Hall. All off limits by silent consent.
    Sometime in the wee hours, distant sirens seemed to wake a couple of the students from their stupor. They jumped up, muttered an apology, then headed out the door to their car. A bit odd, but no one seemed interested. An hour or so later the rest of the party swigged the dregs of their beers and staggered home. Sirens were again wailing from the direction of campus.
    By full daylight Sunday morning we were hearing rumors from campus along with more sirens. A hook and ladder from Marion screamed past on the nearby highway. The oldest building on campus, Old Main, was burning.
    The Southern Illinoisan newspaper was already out on the streets and on our front step, so the printed news of the fire would have to wait until Monday morning. Instead we read about Nixon at Midway for talks about ending the conflict in Viet Nam

while some of the fiercest fighting of the war went on. Monday gave us the full picture of our own campus war.

The fire in Old Main had been started in a dozen places on the third and fourth floors. Discovered by maintenance foreman, Bob Browner, at 7:50 am Sunday, the blaze quickly grew despite the fact that fire crews were on the scene almost immediately. Their hoses would not reach to the fourth floor and the top of the ladder truck's ladder became entangled in the large trees surrounding the building.

On the ground students and staff from nearby dorms were recruited to carry files, books, manuscripts, art work, and furnishings from the offices and class rooms of the burning building. Thirty at a time were allowed on the flaming third floor to retrieve whatever they could carry.

By 9:15 am the entire fourth floor was engaged and the first of the towers collapsed. There was no hope for the landmark building and salvage operations ceased until the fire was totally extinguished. After finding numerous starter points for the fire on the third and fourth floors along with obscene messages scrawled on the walls the fire was declared arson.

The tent city near the art department disappeared that week as did the more vocal of the draft protestors. I never again saw the two students who left our party early.

The Big Muddy River Bridge

When we moved to the country, we found our nearest neighbor was an old steel truss bridge over the Big Muddy River. The bridge was rusty and twisted with a plank floor that rumbled like thunder when a vehicle drove across it. Twice a year floods with great loads of debris had weakened and bent the bridge. Many contacts with cars and trucks driven home from the tavern on the other side added to the damage.

We had little reason to cross the bridge except to vote at the township polling place in Sand Ridge. We could have driven around, but that was a twenty-five mile trip compared to the half mile at the river crossing. Not too many people feared the decrepit bridge enough to take the roundabout route.

A few years later a study of the county bridges resulted in a grading system. On a scale of 'A to E' we rated an 'E.' 'E's' fell into the 'must be closed immediately' category. Until the county found a workable way to close the bridge and figure out alternate routes, the school bus driver had to stop the bus, unload the students, drive across the bridge, then walk back across the bridge, and escort the kids to the bus.

All of this nonsense was arrived at because an empty school bus was listed at six tons and a loaded bus at eleven tons. How could the addition of a dozen small children add up to five tons? A better way of looking at this is to say if the bus goes down with the bridge, no children would be lost.

In the meantime the county replaced some of the planking on the doomed bridge. All of the new planks had disappeared by the following morning. An emergency board meeting was held and a vote on plans for a new bridge passed. It would be built downstream a half mile and the old bridge would remain open until its completion. The soybean field to the east of us became a construction zone.

The construction company must have been someone's brother-in-law because they went to work immediately. They hired no flaggers, provided no detours or even signs. We just drove through the mess to the main road as best we could. Fortunately the operators of the graders and earth movers were a polite and considerate bunch. Not once did they mow down a befuddled driver on their way to work or grocery store.

While the construction work progressed, a few new planks appeared on the old bridge decking from time to time and a neighbor's new barn took shape. That project finished, someone else decided his garage needed a new floor. School let out for summer break, and another neighbor hired a water truck to keep the construction dust at bay. Life chugged on for Sand Ridge Township.

The new bridge had one flaw. Actually two. First, it went under water when the Big Muddy River flooded. Someone had made an error when they figured out how tall the bridge had to be. Second, the bridge had no super structure and was almost impossible to see when it was covered with water. Many a fuzzy headed driver coming home from the tavern missed the bridge and drove into the river. No one ever died from these plunges into the muddy water, but it was hard on the vehicles and law enforcement wasted a good many hours looking for drivers who had bailed and walked home.

With the new bridge open and functioning, the old one had to come down. That proved to be a very interesting bit of summer entertainment. Blow torches and sledge hammers were the main tools used. The super structure was slowly detached from the body of the bridge. Long before that part of the job was finished I could see those steel girders swaying in the wind. Instead of a bridge that thundered, we now had one the groaned and clanged.

The last day the super structure reigned over the neighborhood, the workers took their places like usual and I took my place on the river bank to watch. My neighbor on the other side of the bridge approach, however, untied his boat and cranked up the motor to watch the work from a position in the middle of the river.

One worker climbed to the top of the bridge to cut a last girder holding the bridge aloft. One cut and the whole thing collapsed into the river, worker, blow torch, and all. When the mess settled, my neighbor steered his boat into the debris and pulled the worker from the water. The man was mostly unhurt, just a bit embarrassed by his mistake. By the end of the day the remains of the old bridge were gone.

80

Pot Flights over Nile Creek
Or Where's the Weed

Out there in the bend of the Big Muddy River we were very isolated. Only a gravel road connected us with the rest of the world. We did have a ten party phone line that was mostly busy all day. A few cars including the broke down old Buick the mailman drove passed the end of our quarter mile driveway. The only overhead traffic was the Life Flight helicopter on its way to the emergency room of the Cape Girardeau hospital. And that didn't happen very often.

The quiet of isolation was broken one morning. I was washing up the milk buckets and strainer, when the silence was split up the middle by a racket greater than ten freight trains passing by. The dishes in the cupboard rattled; the knick-knacks on the piano danced; the dogs set up a terrific howling and the poor chickens crashed against the sides of their wire pen.

Grabbing a dish towel for my dripping hands, I ran out into the yard. A rackety old helicopter was just dipping out of sight behind the trees. As I stood listening and expecting the noise to die out, it increased. The chopper had turned to make another pass over my clearing. Like a scene from the A-Team I found myself staring up at the underside of the aircraft.

A clear panel in the belly of the craft revealed a man peering down at me. When the chopper reached the trees, it climbed again and swooped off to turn for another pass over my clearing. Back and forth a dozen times and I finally figured out they were flying a grid pattern.

What were these buggers doing anyway. The helicopter was clearly an old issue army craft straight out of the Viet Nam era or a bad movie set. It would not have been surprising if it suddenly began producing bursts of machine gun fire.

Our 200 acres were right at the meeting of four sections. The chopper was apparently scrutinizing the landscape a section at a time, so we got a quadruple dose of their attention.

After terrorizing me and the livestock for a suitable length of time it flew off to run a grid over the next clearing. This went on all day, then stopped. Until the next run three weeks later.

After asking a million questions of assorted people I discovered the flyovers were drug agency people hunting for marijuana plots. Southern Illinois had been an official producer of hemp for Navy rope during World War II. Left unattended at war's end, the hemp continued to grow in the clearings year after year.

In the 1970's smoking pot became popular and enterprising locals were adept at prompting the struggling hemp plants into full production. More commercial minded folk got involved and the pot trade flourished. All fueled by the bootleg grow in the hills.

Taking a hike through the woods became problematic when growers began guarding their crop from energetic students from nearby Southern Illinois University. Meeting up with an armed guard or a slobbering dog in the middle of the forest was a sobering experience.

The patrols continued through the summer and early fall. I still waved my dish towel and screamed at them. Fat lot of good that did. It earned me a wave and a thumbs up from the guy in the belly of the chopper. The dogs and chickens adapted and barely noticed the racket overhead. Then it was over. That year's pot harvested and stowed away.

Buddy-Buddy and the Black Bull

Our part of down state Illinois was home to several home grown criminals. Or maybe they were slightly shady, slick-Dick type businessmen. In either case they were pretty scary guys. Buddy-Buddy controlled the cigarette vending business for the entire region and had his finger in the cattle market pie when I met up with him.

We literally met over a cow or rather our black bull. Buddy had leased the vacant farm that adjoined the very back of our place. The fence was good and Buddy's cows were a scrawny lot he had received as part payment on an usurious loan.

Cows being cows did cow things and in the end our black bull hopped the fence and made whoopee with Buddy's cows. The first I knew of it was the appearance of a slick Dick of a guy banging on my door threatening mayhem. He had a gun stuck in his waistband.

In my best harassed housewife voice I told him I would take care of it, but it was a long walk to that back pasture. He asked if he could drive there and I told him, no. Big gulley with no bridge.

He fumed and threatened, paced the narrow strip of concrete in front of my door, then stalked back to his car and drove off.

The next I heard from Buddy-buddy was a phone call threatening a lawsuit for damage to his cows. I told him I would sue for the breeding fees to my bull. At $100 a hump that would add up since I had counted at least 28 cows in his rented pasture. Maybe I would throw in a couple more for good measure.

Buddy-Buddy muttered a string of very bad words, then hung up. I never heard from him again and the scrawny cows disappeared from the back pasture by week's end.

Fire with fire. What's good for the goose is good for the gander. And all those related platitudes. Good riddance my granny would say.

Dog or Doorbell

    Before we moved to the country a dozen uninvited people dinged our doorbell every week. They were selling knives, perfume, lotions, shoes, storm windows, guttering, insurance, tickets to school and community events. It was endless. And they all wanted to come in the house to plead their case.
    I would stand on the stoop, tell them not interested, and retreat. Still they were an intrusion and a waste of time.
    When we moved to an isolated place in the country, I expected such doorbell dingers to cease. For one thing we had no doorbell and the door was protected by a sturdy, locked storm door. For another the driveway was long and rutted. In summer it was hard to tell there was even a house back there in the bushes.
    Still I had no luck shedding the door to door crowd. Religious nuts and politicians joined the parade. No matter how unwelcoming I treated them, they continued to bother me.
    Then one day it stopped. Weeks without a single intruder bumping up my driveway, pounding on the door, peering in my windows. Maybe the word had got out and they had finally given up.
    A whole year passed without a single stranger confrontation. Then one day I came home to find our dog tied to the hydrant out front. Odd, because all the country dogs ran free. There were no lease laws and our dog didn't even have a collar. It seemed unnecessary. Our nearest neighbors were so far away they were out of sight. Likewise the twisty gravel road.
    A length of electrical wire had been wrapped around his neck and secured to the hydrant pipe. A clue! Must have been an inspector or repairman from the rural electric company. Another

piece to the puzzle came when I overheard the volunteers at the polling place across the river talking about a dog, while I filled out my ballot. Mean bugger, they said. Stay away from that place.

After filling out a few more boxes on the ballot I realized the dog they were discussing was mine. My gray wire-haired beast with clipped ears and tail.

The humane society had offered the standard Schnauzer to us for free when we showed up looking for a tough dog. He was a bit too tough and had been relegated to a cage with a huge Great Dane after nearly killing his previous cage mates. Turns out he had been there for over six months. I figured they were exaggerating, but who can turn down free.

Bart did his job though and kept the neighborhood dog packs, coyotes, and wandering farm dogs away. He was too much of a loner to join up with any of them. Turns out he also kept the doorbells dingers away. His favorite tactic was the snarling, I'm right behind you approach. Apparently he had developed quite an audience over the months he had come to live with us. His reputation persisted and out lived him by many years. Thirty years to be exact. Zero door-to-door salesmen.

When we moved to a house in a small town on the Strait of Juan de Fuca, I figured the door bell dingers would descend once again and they did. Not wanting another dog, especially in town, I tried other methods. A 'No Soliciting' sign had no effect. Ignoring the chirrupy door bell drove me nuts and I never did figure out how to disconnect it.

I finally ordered a big molded dragon holding a sign that read 'Unwelcome' and installed him next to the front door. It seemed to help. He didn't need to be fed either.

Black Suits And Other Front Door Visitors

The Internal Revenue Guys

It was a perfectly normal Southern Illinois morning down on the farm. The livestock had been fed, milked, petted, and whatever else was needed. My husband was off to his morning lectures at the university and I was looking forward to a second cup of coffee and a couple of rounds of Mario Brothers or the Adventures of Link.

I was still debating which game should enliven my morning break when a very large, very black car pulled into my driveway. Now what? Everyone I knew on the hill drove a broke down pickup truck or a ruptured Buick.

I went out to intercept the interloper. I was not in the habit of letting just anyone into the house. When I reached the driveway I saw that the interloper was plural. Two buggers in the black car that was purring in my gravel drive.

One got out—black suit, brief case, and attitude. Not good. I should have gone shopping. Too late now.

Black suit was unwilling to conduct business in the carport and pushed past me to the front door. Said he was from the IRS. Really? Proof man, proof. Unfortunately he had plenty.

Once inside he looked around for a place to spread out his papers. A place with some light. The kitchen table was the only choice. Crap. I would have to disinfect the place when he left. Assuming he planned on leaving. The sooner the better.

He finally got down to business. It was with great relief that I realized it wasn't my business he was getting down on. Homer Bacon, he said. You bought some pigs from Homer Bacon last year.

A couple of culls was all we bought in the pig line last year, I told him. Cull weaner pigs.

He laid out copies of the check I had written to Homer and detailed the problem. This payment was not declared on Mr. Bacon's income tax form, he said. I looked at the copy of my check. It was made out to Homer Bacon and it said 2 pigs in the left hand corner. I found my check book and showed him the carbon of my check. Identical. No hanky panky in that direction.

By then my brain was grinding out the solution to this problem. I did not want to get Homer in any more trouble than he already was.

Homer Bacon, yes, but not the son. I bought the pigs from his father.

That seemed safe. Homer Senior was close to 90 years old though he was spry as 25 year old. And he lived on the farm with his son. Yes. The old guy I repeated.

The agent seemed deflated. It was one less link to the crimes of the son. I looked at the check again. Forty bucks for two weaner pigs. For this they send TWO black suited agents miles out in the country to bug me. I waved him out of my house and scrubbed the table down with disinfectant.

The Turquoise Blue Chevy Hood

We hadn't lived on the hill farm out on the Big Muddy River more than a year or two before we started having trouble with our septic system. A plumber friend unclogged things a couple of times, then decided we should dig up the tank and see what was going on.

The digging revealed an old fashioned steel tank with a cover that had rusted through and collapsed. A new tank wasn't a real solution. For one thing steel tanks had become obsolete and we would need major digging to install one of the huge concrete tanks. Money, Money, Money!

Since the tank itself seemed to be in good shape, we decided we needed only a lid. Of course such creatures did not exist. Every steel tank in the country probably had a rusted lid.

With a bit of plotting we figured out that the opening was about the size of a car hood. And guess what? We had several to choose from. Living out at the end of the earth we had no garbage pickup and the county disposal site required an expensive dump license. Previous dwellers on our 140 acres had simply dumped their trash and worn out stuff in the gulley behind the house. At least two old cars resided in the trash heap.

With a bit of cussing and sweat the hood of a 1957 Chevy parted company with its car body. The turquoise blue hood looked down right jaunty atop our septic tank. It was almost a crime to cover it up, but it solved our plumbing problem for a good ten years after that.

The Black Boys and My Broken Muffler

Just as I left Carbondale for the drive home, my 1973 Dodge Dart started clanking like crazy. Probably not so odd since the car was way past its prime and plagued with a series of difficulties.

I pulled over to the shoulder, got out and looked the car over. The muffler and tail pipe assembly had come loose at the forward end and was jabbing into the road. Yikes. No wonder it was making so much noise.

I decided to drive the five miles to the next town where I usually had the car serviced rather than try find a place to cross the highway to turn around.

As I walked back around the car, I noticed another car had pulled up behind me. An old blue caddy with a half dozen young black men in it. I waved, shrugged, and climbed into my not so trust worthy Dart. When I pulled back onto the highway, they followed.

We made a very slow procession down the highway. The boys hung out the windows of the caddy and waved traffic around us. They cheered and whistled when I sped up and made the sparks fly. I tried not to notice the track I was engraving into the warm blacktop.

The muffler hung on bravely and we finally reached the intersection into Murphysboro. I signaled my turn to the auto body shop, the crew in the caddy honked, cheered, then waited through the light to be sure I made it.

Guardian angels come in all shapes and colors.

The Journey of a Zinc Plate Etching

The small knot of seniors and grad students working in the printing labs on the top floor of Allan Hall were miles away in their philosophy of life from the potters and sculptors in the basement.

In our elevated space we dealt with fairly precise two dimensional renderings of landscapes and the models who posed for the drawing classes. Work on a thirty pound litho stone or acid applications to the zinc plates was tedious and precise. We had little congress with each other or the other art students outside of class and lab work.

By contrast the basement dwellers ranted and raved as they flung their gobs of clay around. Others routinely skipped class to march in protest of the Viet Nam War or slashed out three dimensional wood sculptures of huddled figures. One teacher was working on a larger than life parade of welded steel figures meant to march across the library gardens in protest.

As the year progressed, many of those students moved into a tent city on the lawn so their anti war banners and chants could reach a larger audience. They began to focus on the draft and the military when several of them received their notice to report to their draft boards.

Meanwhile, us printers ignored world events and prepared work for a show in a newly opened gallery in the Old Main building across the way from us. An exciting opportunity to show off our prints and drawings.

Though it was neither intentional, nor recognized, our work was as much a protest as the gaudy show put on by our counterparts in the basement. Desolation and despair were the overtones of nearly all of the art we presented.

Single figures bent over with heavy loads struggling along empty roads to infinity. Edward Munch-like screams howling from distorted mouths. Not a one of us presented anything radiating peace or happiness. Yet we still looked down on the basement dwellers and their grim representations of life.

The show had been in place for only a few weeks when the building was torched by unidentified protestors. Not because of our insignificant art work of course. Rather it was the very forward presence of the historic building as well as the shooting range on the fourth floor. A few art works were retrieved from the gallery before smoke and falling beams drove the salvage workers back. Most of us counted our work lost.

Fast forward from 1969 to 2016. A long 47 years and a lot of living later I'm sitting at my computer hunting for information on a set of botanical illustrations I had worked on while still at Southern Illinois University. Up came a listing for an etching with my name on it for sale at a Chicago gallery.

The bent, unhappy, shrieking figure demanded a closer look. The tiny picture was matted and framed in a most professional manner and it was marked 'sold.' It had to be my picture from the burning building because I had never made another print from that particular plate.

I contacted the lady who owned the gallery and found that she had sold another of my prints a few months earlier. The lady who brought the prints into her gallery was on a cruise and unreachable. All quite amazing. I hunted up an old portfolio of my prints and drawings from the era and mailed them to her. Maybe she could squeeze some cash from them to help her new gallery venture.

She accepted them and began the process of sorting, matting, and framing them. In return she promised to track down the woman who brought her the first two art works. I'm still waiting.

The Great Wall and the Camel

In 1994 we went to China for a mathematics conference in Changchun. Of course we spent a week in Beijing before flying on to the conference. Who in their right mind would fly halfway around the world and waste such an opportunity.

The second morning we went off on a tour provided as part of our airline ticket package. Usually we shunned tours, but this one had perks not usually open to casual travelers. Or so they said.

Stop one was the Great Wall. It must have been the back alley of the Wall because the huge parking lot was nearly empty. Good for us. No long lines to buy a ticket for the privilege of trekking up those tall stone steps and an empty café.

The wall itself was spectacular. We were right at the end of that stretch of the wall because the view from the top revealed long lines of workers moving rocks and debris by hand in an effort to restore another section of this world treasure.

Heat lay like a blanket over the whole treeless region and seemed magnified by the wall. We soon descended to search out a cooler spot. Crossing the parking lot to the café we spotted a large camel tied in the shade of the lone tree.

He was a two hump camel wearing a tasseled head dress and a red rug with cut outs for his humps as a saddle. Clumps of long silky hair and bare spaces over his shoulders and rump made me think of horses brought from cooler regions and clipped to make them more able to stand the heat. Perhaps this beast normally lived in a cooler region. Or maybe he just had a skin problem. In any case he wasn't bringing in any money for his handler.

The stooped, turban wearing fellow sat cross-legged on the ground smoking up a storm and paying no attention to passing tourists debarking from a nearby bus. We hurried past and entered the dark cavern of the café.

We ordered coffee and a diet soda in a can. We had been warned to avoid bottled liquids because the Chinese were adept at refilling used bottles with unknown and possibly unsafe liquids. We found a table close to the door where we could watch our bus and the camel. Soon a lady with a little girl came across the parking lot and made a bee line for the camel.

Dressed in a billowy dress and stilty heels with a huge yellow handbag over her arm, the lady seemed out of place among the shorts, back packs, and running shoes of the other visitors. The little girl looked right at home though with her shorts and a t-shirt with a sports team logo on the front.

The smoking man tossed his smoke and hurried to prod his camel into alertness. He hauled a portable stairway to the camel's side, tied the lead rope to its rail, and motioned to the pair.

The girl scooted up the rickety stair to perch between the camel's humps. The mother made a slower ascent, but was soon perched behind her daughter. The camel man produced an old Polaroid camera and snapped a picture. By then I was right behind him snapping as many photos as possible before anyone could react. I gave the mother-daughter pair a short wave and retreated to the tour bus.

The mother handed the camel man some bills and disappeared back across the parking lot. The camel man stowed the stairway and resumed his post in the shade to smoke another cigarette. A Camel perhaps? None of the trio seemed to pay any attention to the Great Wall that towered over them.

Camel By the Highway

Out here on the Olympic Peninsula livestock along the highway are pretty rare. A cow or two, some exotic sheep, maybe even a llama, but a camel? Here in the home of very tall trees, deer and bear, camels are few and far between. In fact the one that lives between Port Angeles and Sequim might be the only one, ever.

I was used to camels by the side of the road when I lived in the Black Hills because of the famous Passion Play that brought tourists by the bus load to our tiny town of Spearfish. You can't have a Passion Play without camels.

The founder of our claim to fame, Joseph Smith, had a ranch nestled up to the state highway that led from Belle Fourche to the north into the center of town. When the camels weren't working, they could be seen wandering in the pastures alongside the road.

My cousin sometimes had a part in the play as a camel helper. He wore a long bathrobe and trotted alongside the reluctant beasts with a whippy stick to keep them on the track through the drama going on around them. Another boy held the lead rope and ran on ahead.

Since the pageant was held at night, the requirements for costume, makeup, and acting ability were pretty low. Just don't let go of the camel. Good advice for anyone with or without a camel appearing in an outdoor amphitheater in front of hundreds of people. Hang on.

But what about that camel out on Highway 101 on the Olympic Peninsula? He was a shaggy beast, a bit smaller than the majestic creatures in Spearfish. He lived in a rocky pasture with a herd of dwarf sheep and a long eared donkey. His job was a few notches down the scale of importance too. Mostly he entertained at birthday parties and ambled around street fairs and parades. A camel for hire.

And, like the camel at the Great Wall, you could pay your shekels and climb aboard for a photo op. When he wasn't working, he would stand around with a tweak of hay sticking out of both sides of his mouth.

Where did the poor fellow come from? Can you buy a camel on the internet? Turns out you can. A bred female goes for about $13,000, while a gelded male will set you back a paltry $4000. Of course you will also need an appropriate saddle, halter, lead rope, and assorted shots and supplements. The two hump variety is good for cold regions, but costs more. Who knew?

The Girl On the Trolley Roof

Here I am—headed to visit one of the world's premier universities. I'm in a huge black car being driven by a man in spiffy suit, cap, and tie who looks like a movie mafia boss. The streets of Changchun are spotless. The chaos of the flight and the domestic airports only a bad memory. The hotel awaits.

Then I spot a girl in the traffic lane next to us. The girl is on the roof of a street car. Quit literally, outside and perched on the roof of the street car racing along its steel rails on the route from the airport into the city.

We had flown into Beijing in late May. We had a busy week visiting the sights and treasures of the city and surrounding countryside including the Great Wall, the Forbidden City, the Summer Palace, and the Ming Tombs before flying to Changchun for the business part of our journey.

Like many of the modern parts of China, the airport in Changchun looked exactly like the domestic airport in Beijing. And in Shanghai. And in Hefei. One blueprint for all.

We walked the long, bare concourse to the exit hall where a large crowd of people waited behind the barriers. We quickly spied a big hulk of a guy with a sign bearing our names. He stood out because most of the crowd were a head or more shorter and wore faded gray. He was our transportation to the Friendship Guest House. We ducked under the rope separating the arriving passengers and their greeters to join him.

Outside at the curb our car awaited us, long, big, and black. With a lot of honking and fist shaking we made it out of the airport to the long boulevard leading into the city. That's when we encountered a city street car.

Street cars travel along a set of steel rails set in the roadway. They are powered by electricity from lines strung above their routes. The connector is a long rod called a trolley pole, hence the common name of trolley for a street car.

Something had gone awry with this particular street car. The temporary fix was a human one. A young girl crouched on its roof holding the trolley pole in place kept the car rolling to its destination. Her grey tunic flapped with the speed of the car and her long black hair wrapped itself around her face. She had much more to worry about.

Though the route was fairly straight, the car rocked from side to side and its stops and starts added acceleration and deceleration to the mix. The pole was obviously unwieldy and the girl was small. Add to this the shower of sparks that drenched her every time the pole slipped.

As a major intersection with overhead wires everywhere approached, I could see her stiffen and shift her grip on the trolley pole. She was going to change course. Only one thing filled her mind and that was catching the correct line to send the street car out of the square in the desired direction.

The girl stood taller and caught her lower lip in her teeth. Her head was only a few inches from the bare power lines. She swayed slightly to the left and flicked the pole under a maze of wires to catch the power for next leg of the trip.

The lurch of the street car's change of direction brought the girl to her knees, but she kept the trolley pole in place. The last I saw of her was the flapping of her gray tunic.

When I sat back in the plush seat, our host, who had noted my attention to the street car, had one comment. 'Nonstop to main square.'

What about child labor and human rights?

Yellow Mountain

We were living in the University guest house in Hefei, China while my husband was giving a series of mathematical lectures. Though we were only about an hour's flight from Shanghai and Hefei is a huge city, conditions were pretty primitive. Stripped down living you could call it.

Our hosts did all sorts of things to make us comfortable, but it is always hard to figure out what another person wants or needs. Especially if you are dealing with people from opposite ends of the earth with very little common language. Still, we were all stuttering along.

Until our hosts had a meeting in Beijing for the weekend and decided we should have a weekend away too. They booked us a flight to Huangshan without asking. Huangshan is really Yellow Mountain. The one place in China I did not want to visit. It was the destination of choice for mountaineers, dare devils, and people unafraid of heights, narrow trails, sheer drop offs. People who did not mind a ten mile walk after a perilous ascent in a basket up to the top of the mountain to their hotel. A hotel with none of the finer comforts like running water and real beds.

We had talked about it before we left home because it was less than an hour's flight from Hefei. We knew the Chinese were in love with that wild region of their country. For centuries their artists had painted the jagged mountains until they became symbols of everything Chinese.

But it is very hard to argue with people when you had so little common language. And the plane tickets were non-refundable. Maybe the city that served as the starting point of the trip up the mountain would prove to be interesting. A student drove us to the Hefei airport the next day.

A driver straight out of a Mafia movie picked us up at the Huangshan airport. He was accompanied by a wimpy looking guy who introduced himself as our guide, Ray. The car was big and black and polished inside and out. They drove us to a hotel in downtown. It looked good from the outside, but it was all downhill from there.

The lobby was shabby and filled with dirty overstuffed chairs and a truck load of head high cloisonné vases. The elevator was dim and the upstairs hallway just plain dark. Dark, smelly, and noisy. The room was worse. One bed was soggy soft and sank to the floor when you even dared look at it. The other one must have had a granite mattress.

Breakfast was warm steamed bread, a few bad dumplings, a pickled thing, and a bowl of thin rice gruel. I skipped it all, put instant coffee in my tea and ate a Snickers bar from my pack.

We gathered up our few belongings and waited outside for our guide. He showed up at nine sharp with a different driver, a brother of yesterday's driver. The car was newly washed and waxed and already showing rain drops.

We told our guide, Ray, that we needed to change hotels. He replied 'No need. You have reservations on the mountain top.'

'Absolutely not,' we said. Ray mumbled into his phone for awhile, then says he has made a reservation at a 'good' hotel, but we can't check in until later. In the meantime we must go to the mountain and 'Just look at it.'

Under black clouds that threatened to send enough rain to wash us down river we drove out of town. The countryside was a marvelous panorama of terraced farm land planted to rape which produces canola oil. The rape was in full bloom with bright yellow flowers. Workers were plowing the fallow fields next to the rape with water buffalo. It was more picturesque than any art print or travelogue. Maybe this jaunt would be okay after all.

After about an hour's drive we pulled into the parking lot of the obligatory gift shop. This one featured huge cloisonné vases, but we had learned long ago to head straight to the rest rooms. They were always Western style, well equipped, and spotless.

A few minutes after we returned to the car, the clouds churned out their first blast of rain, thunder, and lightening, but there was no turning back. The driver muscled on. We were soon in the mountains enveloped by the clouds themselves. Traffic on the steep switch back road was bumper to bumper tour buses, bicycles, and backpackers.

By the time we reached the cable car terminal visibility was zero. Ray insisted we get out and join the crowd lined up for tickets. He demanded our passports and ran off to buy tickets. Was the little bugger thinking about hog tying us and dragging us to the gondola? We actually went through the turnstile where we found a mass of waiting riders and one hole in the floor toilet. Also a sign saying there would be a three hour wait for the next trip up the mountain.

We bolted for the exit gate. Ray finally capitulated and took our tickets to try for a refund. We stood waiting in the pouring rain rejoicing. On his return we hiked through the woods to a nearby hotel. Ray babbled into his cell phone the whole way. The hotel was warm and clean and had an excellent restaurant. Also a clean western style toilet.

The trip down the mountain was totally fog bound. We couldn't see past the hood ornament on the black car, but we were content. No matter what old Ray had in store for us, it had to be better. And that is another story.

The Three Line System

In 1985 Szeged, Hungary was still under Soviet control. Though it was a fairly large city, it was still a pretty bleak place. In many ways living there was like going back in time to the early 1900's.

There were very few cars on the streets and those few shared the wide streets with horse drawn wagons. Every few blocks a man or woman worked at sweeping the street and sidewalk with brooms made of twigs. No one picked up the debris and the next day they swept it up again.

Most of the stores used the three line system which had several variations. They all added up to control. The most severe pattern was the counter only approach to shopping. When the shopper came in the one and only door to the shop, they were met with a counter across the entire room. You were expected to approach the right hand clerk and tell them what you wanted. Next you went to the middle clerk to pay, then to the last remaining clerk to present your receipt and pick up your wrapped purchase.

In a slightly less restrictive system the shopper was allowed to examine the choices before selecting something. Then the clerk sent the shopper to pay and then pick up the wrapped parcel.

Some shops actually allowed the shopper to examine the goods, but only a chosen number of shoppers were allowed in at any one time. You picked up an obligatory basket at the door and followed a set pattern through the store aisles. This did not change whether there was one shopper or twenty. At check out your basket was emptied and you received a receipt which you presented to another clerk. You paid her and went through a third line to pick up your purchase.

Your purchase was wrapped in brown paper and tied with string. No bags here—plastic or paper and no tape. Clerking often ended up being an exercise in dexterity.

I was in line in a very small shop with narrow aisles one day when the woman ahead of me changed her mind about buying something in her basket and turned around to go back to replace it on the shelf. A clerk and the other shoppers protested and insisted she keep moving forward. She got agitated and seemed on the verge of making a scene.

Afraid of the mess and bother that might ensue, I took the small dish from her hand and placed it in my own basket. Better to spend fifty cents, than to wait through endless harangues in Hungarian. There was no other easy escape.

Train Rules

We were traveling from Budapest to Vienna one Fall morning in 1985. At that time Hungary was still firmly under the control of the Soviet Union and our excursions were closely monitored. Entrance and exit papers were required and our passports had to be stamped for each night we spent away from our apartment in Szeged.

We had the first class car to ourselves and were looking forward to the excellent coffee and pastries served on the short journey.

Some thirty miles down the track, a back packing student entered the car from second class and made himself at home. The conductor followed shortly. He checked our passes and moved on to the student. The fellow handed him his ticket and sat back with his feet on the opposite seat.

The conductor politely asked the scruffy fellow why he was in first class when his pass only allowed second class. And remove your feet from the seat, please.

No one here, man. Second class is full.

The conductor gestured to the rear of the car, but was ignored. He bent down and knocked the offending feet from the seat, then grabbed the back of the student's shirt with one hand, his backpack in the other.

Up, ordered the conductor. He shoved the pack at the guy, then pulled the stop signal. While the train slowed to a stop, he escorted the student to the door. The screech of wheels subsided. The door was opened. The steps partially unfolded. The conductor lifted and pushed the offender to the ground. Not a person nor a building in sight.

You can't leave me out here.

The conductor answered by retracting the steps and closing the door. The train moved on. Rules were more than rules in the Soviet system.

The Not So Royal, Royal Hotel

In 1985 Szeged, Hungary had one hotel in the downtown area. If there were others in outlying parts of town, I never saw them. The Hotel Royal was a relic of Szeged's Art Nouveau rebuilding. In the spring of 1879 an enormous flood overwhelmed the city. Only a few outlying buildings survived.

With donations from the rest of the world and the genius of a renowned Art Nouveau artist/architect, Ede Magyar, the city was rebuilt. The Votive Church, the University, and the Hotel Royal were all part of the 'new' Szeged. Many of the old buildings were decorated with flowing roof lines and fanciful figures.

We were living in Szeged so we had no need of a hotel, but every now and then we felt like a break from our own cooking. The dining room of the Royal was one of the few choices within walking distance of our apartment.

The entrance to the Royal was a nondescript doorway much like all the others on the street. No big sign, no flashing neon lights, just a small plaque with its name and street number. Inside was another world.

Heavy drapes, high ceilings, and gilt trim spoke of the old days of Hungarian dominance, of the reception of high ranking visitors from Vienna, of formal balls and state dinners.

The lady at the reception desk pushed a pen across to us, then retrieved it when we indicated we were only interested in eating. She led us to the huge dining room and roused the attendant from his nap on a velvet settee. He dusted himself off and straightened his cuffs and tie.

Offered our choice of tables, we selected a small one near the window. He handed us large leather-bound menus, but indicated we should ignore them in favor of the tattered sheet of typed menu choices. It didn't make much difference to us because it was all in Hungarian.

Quick to react, the sleepy looking fellow suggested the daily special of schnitzel and potatoes or perhaps the Hasenpfeffer. He favored us with a broad grin when we chose the schnitzel. Probably the only dish in the kitchen that day as it was quickly set before us.

Even the potatoes were greasy, but we ate it all and washed it down with some very foul mineral water. The grinner brought the check and we gave him a substantial tip. Next time we would try the Hasenpfeffer.

And the next time the grinner met us at the door and escorted us to 'our' table. The Hasenpfeffer seemed to be ground up schnitzel in gravy, but then when dining out halfway around the world in a small Soviet controlled city, beggars can't be choosers applies.

We ate there several more times during our six month stay in Szeged with the same results. I never saw another diner in the place.

The Hotel Royal Again.

1996, ten years after our first visit to the Hotel Royal we were back in Szeged for a week. We spent the first night in the pre-arranged accommodations at the Academy of Science. The room faced West and became a hot box by bedtime. No fan and no air conditioning. Come morning we found our breakfast laid out on a table in the hallway outside our room. It consisted of a huge silver tray with pots of hot water, cold water, and sugar, two cups, and a tea bag. A plate of pimento loaf with two round rolls and butter made up the edible portion of breakfast.

We packed up and fled down the street to the Hotel Royal. Vastly improved under private ownership. We checked in, then had a real breakfast. It was a buffet with granola, yogurt, fresh squeezed juice in three colors, Kiwi, peach, cherry, and apricot. Good coffee, rolls, jam, eggs, cheese, salami, a staple in all of Eastern Europe, peppers, and sour cream.

The room was less than wonderful, but did have air conditioning. Szeged had made many improvements in our ten year absence. There was even a McD's just a few doors down. We met many old friends from across the world. Each one had a favorite place to eat so we didn't eat other meals at the Royal until the last day of the meeting.

The Academy held their banquet in the gilt and velvet dining room of the Royal. And it did look royal on that occasion. Everyone had on their best duds, the lighting was perfect, the room spotless. As we were escorted to our table, I spied a familiar face across the room. The grinner still worked at the Royal.

He grinned even wider when he saw me and sprinted across the room to take over the escort duties from his work mate. Ten years and thousands of miles later we had a mini reunion. Two grins, a flourish or two, and we were settled at our place at the banquet table. No honored guest ever received such attention.

Long Ride To Lisbon 1986

In the summer of 1986 we were living in Madrid. We had an apartment just up the hill from the Prado and though there were enough sights and experiences in and around Madrid to keep a person busy for years, we were pleased to find a reason to visit Lisbon. A math meeting of course.

Uncomfortably we allowed a helpful friend, a Madrid resident, to arrange our train tickets. He bought second class seats. Unless you are a poverty stricken student, do not travel second class on long train journeys.

Though the traffic was the usual wild mess, our taxi driver managed and deposited us at the station in good time. The second class car was a bare bones affair with hard seats facing each other four by four down a narrow aisle.

We settled ourselves in forward facing seats mid-car and waited. Soon a grandmother with a young girl and numerous bundles joined us. We were knee to knee with a ten hour forty-three minute ride before us.

It could have been worse. The pair of women were neat, polite, and thin. Across the aisle two fat guys in suits and ties wedged themselves into a seats facing a chunk of a football player and his very tall girl friend.

Before the train left the station, a wild haired fellow leaped onto the train with station police trailing. He ignored them and made a passionate speech, then dodged down the aisle collecting donations in his hat. At our seat he ignored us, but pleaded with the grandmother who dropped a few coins in his hat.

When he disappeared into the next car, the grandmother showed us a tattered campaign brochure exhorting voters to be mindful of the plight of the Basques in Northern Spain. She pantomimed marking a ballot and stuffing it into the ballot box.

On June 22 Spain was having a general election. Campaigning was allowed only in the month proceeding balloting and that was a scant month away.

We nodded our understanding and settled ourselves for the long ride. With a lurch the train prepared to leave the station. The wild haired man jumped from the train and stood watching. We waved as we passed him.

The country side was mildly interesting though very arid and tree-less. Long horned skinny cattle wandered through the scrub. We had been told these were the herds that produced the fighting bulls, but even a bull fight every ten minutes year around couldn't use up that many critters. And one good Texas longhorn could have whipped them all with one hoof tied behind his back.

At the border the train finally stopped. Our seatmates picked up their bundles and climbed down. A few new passengers got on, but the train was decidedly lighter. Three young people, two guys and a girl took the seats behind us. They were quiet until the train pulled out of the station, then the party began.

Frequent trips to the stinky toilet at the back of the car to snort, swig, or light up soon had the trio flying. Unfortunately for them it also had them hitch hiking. After several attempts to calm the partiers the conductor called the train to a halt at small village. With the help of the husky guy across the aisle the two guys and their very out of it girlfriend were escorted off the train.

We continued on to Lisbon without incident.

A couple of morals to this story:
1. Buy your own tickets and buy first class.
2. Be nice to wild-eyed strangers in election years.
3. No drinking and drugging on European trains. Behave!

The Dogs of Lisbon

After the ten hour, forty-three minutes train ride from Madrid the St. Apollania Station in Lisbon looked pretty darn good. An enterprising taxi driver met us on the platform and offered his services. We were quickly and efficiently hauled off through mind boggling traffic to our hotel.

In less strained circumstances I might have been unhappy with the hotel, but instead it was a bit of calm in a messy world. The towels were thin and the lights dim, but we had a full view of the city open air market and the elegant Hotel Sheraton loomed in the background.

A quick trip to a nearby grocery supplied tissue, snacks, and two 100 watt light bulbs. We also found the pedestrian walkway under the freeway to the Sheraton. After a bit of sprucing up we made use of this easy access and had supper in the roof top restaurant.

The view from the roof top was spectacular. The entire city seemed to spread out below us. We ate lamb cutlets and river trout. Our hotel looked pretty shabby when we returned, but remembering the two hundred plus dollars we saved by not staying at the upscale hotel helped.

Lisbon sits on several hills guarding the passage of the River Tagus to the Atlantic. Though many of its churches and the main part of the city were destroyed in 1755 by earthquake, fire, and tsunami, it was restored and rebuilt bigger and better.

We spent the first morning at Castle Saint George, then walked through the old Chiado shopping district hunting lunch and marveling over the unique architecture of the buildings erected after the earthquake. From there we climbed the hill to Lisbon Cathedral where several odd, but not unique tombs reside.

A life size stone statue of a man with an ornate sword reclined on the lid of one sarcophagus. Lopo Fernandes Pacheco. His wife and an unknown princess rest nearby. All three have stone dogs at their feet.

Some travel writers give these dogs a warm, furry role to make the whole notion of dead people decorating a place of worship a better feel. Unfortunately these dogs play a different role. Some of them are there to protect the dead from the terrors of the world, but others serve to protect the world from the evil that might emanate from the dead.

After a visit to Lisbon Cathedral we climbed the facing hill to the archeology museum. It is situated in the remains of the Convent of Our Lady of Mt. Carmel with its gothic cathedral that was shaken to its core by the earthquake of 1755. The silence of a museum in the ruins of a vast church is a stark reminder of Lisbon's past. In the earthquake the vaulted ceiling of the cathedral crumbled and fell to earth. Only the pointed stone arches high overhead remained.

The stained glass and rose windows, shattered and broken statuary filled the aisles. Many of these artifacts now stared at us from various displays as we walked through the park-like interior of the old cathedral.

Off the ruined sanctuary, monuments of past knights and ladies greeted us. Carefully carved dogs and lions glared at us. Marble hands, prayer books and swords pulled from the rubble perched on display pedestals.

And what about those dogs? Did they protect their masters from us or were they protecting us from any possible return of their master's souls?

Two years after our visit a huge fire in the main shopping district down the hill from the cathedral destroyed most of the 18th Century buildings. Perhaps one of the stone dogs had gone to sleep on the job and allowed evil to return. Now the people of Lisbon had the opportunity to clean the slate and rebuild their city's heart. Again.

A Splinter of Wood
The Second Crusade

Bits and pieces of the True Cross show up in many churches in many countries. Sometimes it is an actual artifact, various sorts of wood encased in silver or even gold. Other times the relic of the Cross is only a legend or a dim memory. Such a splinter of the True Cross was rumored to be in Nidaros Cathedral in Trondheim, Norway.

Where or if this splinter resided in that cold Northern Norwegian city, I could not find it. They had also lost track of the remains of their local saint, Olaf. If they couldn't locate the body of their beloved king and saint, how could they keep track of a small splinter of wood.

Right around 1000 AD, Christianity as a religion took the same path as a wet behind the ears believer often does. Conquer, spread the good news, jam your new found beliefs down every throat.

The young king of Norway, Sigurd I, was no exception. In 1107 he prepared to sail to the Holy Land for the cause. He managed to raise 5000 men and some 60 ships to do the job. This was an enormous contingent for a small northern country.

In case no one has noticed, Norway is a heck of a long way from Jerusalem. Sigurd made it to England the autumn of the first year. Henry I was king that year and he allowed Sigurd to stay the winter. In the spring of 1108 they again set sail.

That next winter they were in Iberia which is an old name for modern day Spain and Portugal. A local lord in Santiago told them they could stay the winter of 1108. Unfortunately there was not enough food to satisfy the local population and the 5000 interlopers from Norway. Not good.

The local lord cut off the fleet's food—and strong drink—supply. In return Sigurd attacked the castle, robbed, looted, and killed before moving on to Lisbon. Lisbon was one of the ancient world's great cities, half Christian, half heathen.

Sigurd fought another battle against the heathens there, then moved on to Muslim Al-Andalus where they sacked the castle and offered the inhabitants the choice between death and conversion to Christianity. No one took up the offer of baptism. All were killed. Sigurd acquired much treasure.

Other towns along his route suffered similar fates and were left empty of people or treasure as Sigurd fought his way through the Mediterranean. In the spring of 1109 they arrived in Sicily where they were greeted by Count Roger II, a 12 year old. In the summer of 1110 they finally made it to Jerusalem after landing at the port of Acre. The ruling crusader, King Baldwin I, met them at the port and he and Sigurd rode together to the River Jordan, then back to Jerusalem.

Sigurd was given much good stuff including a splinter from the True Cross. The Holy splinter was to be carried to the burial site of St. Olaf in Trondheim. From Acre Sigurd sailed on to Constantinople where he was greeted with open arms by Emperor Alexios I. You can tell how long ago all this stuff happened by the fact that everyone was a 'first.'

When Sigurd made preparations to return to Norway, he decided to go overland and traded his fleet of ships and most of his accumulated loot for many horses. The trip home through Bulgaria, Hungary, Bavaria and a bunch of other countries took him three years and that only got him as far as Denmark. The king there gave him a ship so the journey could be completed.

Ships for horses may have been a bad trade.

Strange Train: Lisbon to Madrid

We left our hotel before 5 am for our trip from Lisbon back to Madrid. We were scheduled to take the same train from the same station, a speedy TER from the venerable St. Apolonia Station on the north bank of the Tagus River. On arrival at the station we found some sort of a problem had developed. We were directed to a shabby, creaky passenger car attached to the back of an empty cattle train.

We shared the car with a group of very drunk young men on their way home from a wedding and a couple from Hong Kong. The Chinese couple spoke good English, but no Spanish or Portuguese. They told us that she was a tour guide and he was a jade dealer on vacation. Another traveler attempted to warn us of a change of trains coming up, but was unable to explain what was going on.

We bumped through some rough empty landscape, then stopped near a little station out in the countryside. With a lot gesturing we were directed to a second train. We climbed down from the first car and hiked across a mess of tracks to a second train waiting on a siding. A short train more ancient than the first. The Chinese couple just followed us.

After an hour or so we pulled into a station where our real train sat waiting for us. A large and obviously well off family boarded just after us. We watched as the spiffily dressed couple with two daughters and several servants settled themselves nearby. They had a ton of baggage which was loaded into the overhead bins by a trio of porters.

The train was clean and roomy by comparison, but had no food or water. When that little fact was announced, the mother and her maid unpacked one of their many bundles and started walking up and down the aisles handing out crackers, candy, grapes and fresh strawberries to the other passengers.

That sustained us until the train made an unscheduled stop at another small station where we were allowed to get a cup of coffee and sandwiches. We arrived in Madrid about 8 pm—about three hours late. A taxi ride back to our apartment at the Magna Villa, a bit of a cleanup, coffee and time to read the Herald Tribune, then off to bed. A very long day and no idea of what disaster had caused the circuitous route home.

Moscow-1992 Rescue

After a damp, chilly beginning our April trip to Moscow turned to nice dry sunshine. We had the cockroaches in the Rossiya Hotel under control and had figured out where a decent, though not exciting meal, could be found.

All of the excitement of the first celebration of Easter in Red Square was over. Dan Rather and his U.S. news crew had packed up and left for the airport a few hours earlier. They had been the only other inhabitants of our section of the hotel other than the floor lady whose job was to sell coffee and hard boiled eggs. And a bunch of armed guys charged with keeping law and order.

The area around Red Square and the Kremlin seemed empty except for a few photographers and vendors selling art work and postcards. Rumor had it that all of the beggars, pickpockets, gypsies, and money changers had been bused some hundreds of miles from the city and dumped. Can't have the riff-raff messing up official doings. We saw the same thing in St. Petersburg at a prestigious athletic event.

But time passes. I was looking at drawings of St. Basil's made by a weathered looking fellow wearing a ball cap lettered USA California when a ratty old bus pulled up at a nearby intersection. Even before it bumped to a stop, the passengers were fighting to be the first off. Whole families loaded with bundles hit the pavement running.

My artist fellow grabbed me by the shoulders, pushed me to the wall and shielded me from the onslaught of thievery occurring as the mob stormed down the street grabbing purses, wallets, shopping bags, and cameras from shoppers and tourists alike.

The riff-raff had returned mad and hungry. I thanked my rescuer and paid him for the drawing I had selected. I indicated my camera and asked him to pose for a photo. He checked to be sure the last of the thieves had left the area, cocked his hat back, and held up the drawing I had purchased and made sure that St. Basils showed over his shoulder. I snapped a few photos and was on my way. One of the high points of my first visit to Russia.

The Boys At The GUM

The three smiling, yet very earnest boys accosted me in the GUM Department store. It was April 1992 and Moscow was gray and slushy both weather wise and politically. Many of the invited participants in the international mathematics meeting we were attending had decided not to risk a visit to Russia at that time. Dan Rather and a scaled down news crew were staying at the same hotel where we were staying.

The GUM would be called a shopping mall in the United States, but in Moscow it was a group of upscale shops united under the banner of the Government Universal Stores. It was and is a huge complex on the street facing Red Square where you could buy the latest shade of lip gloss or an entire bathroom with the finest in tile patterns and gleaming fixtures.

You could also buy Russian goods at controlled prices in the smaller shops tucked away in more obscure corridors. I had bought a jade necklace with the state seal of authenticity for under twenty dollars and a friend had found diamond earrings for a bit less than one hundred dollars. Sheets of collectors stamps were sold in one very small shop at face value. The stick pins with advertising, famous people [mostly Stalin], airlines, schools, the opera and just about every logo in the country fetched a few pennies in another shop. Art books printed in China went for less than four dollars.

Commerce at the state run stores was only in rubles of course. Everyone else dealt in dollars. And everyone was trying hard to make a buck. Out on the street rough looking men sat on folding stools with wooden boxes displaying a few bottles of Coke and perhaps something stronger under cover. Nesting dolls, postcards, knitted scarves, jerry cans of gasoline, even puppies hidden in the folds of warm coats were available for dollars.

The boys at the Gum had perfected a slightly different selling technique. I had watched them for several days before we met. They arrived at the shopping mall shortly after 3:00pm which I presumed was the time school let out. They went to the tiny shop selling pins and buttons, bought a goodly supply, then retired to a dim corner. There they attached the pins to cardboard backing in neat rows. About twenty five pins to a card at a cost of about thirty cents. Finished, they would troop through the Gum looking for potential customers, people with dollars.

On the third day I greeted the boys and was quickly introduced to their wares. All three of them held up their cards of pins and jabbered away in Russian. One reached into his coat and pulled out a nesting doll. The other two had postcards. They ramped up their antics when they saw that I was not about to brush them off and walk away. Punching each other with embarrassment, they did a little song and dance.

I pulled out my camera and indicated a trade. They immediately began posing and settled on leaning together holding up their fingers in rabbit ears. I snapped my photos, then paid three bucks each for three cards of pins. One dollar for each card, two for the photo op. Nine dollars total. We were all very pleased with the deal.

Encounter in a Moscow Bar

As I approached an intersection of the Arbat pedestrian street with a side street used to deliver goods to its many shops, I noticed an old fellow shuffling and snuffling along ahead. His washed gray shirt and pants were as worn as his big hands and poorly shaven cheeks. He must have been one of Moscow's many pensioners living on pennies a day.

While he waited for a large van to pass, he pulled out his handkerchief and applied it to his nose, then crossed the street. I hurried to follow, then saw that he had dropped a pocket knife in the street when he fiddled with his handkerchief.

I picked up the worn knife and called to him with no sign he had heard me. I followed him up the street until he turned into the open door of one of the many bars in the neighborhood. I hesitated before I followed him. This place definitely was off limits to me. A place whose atmosphere and odors warned casual walkers and tourists away. It didn't even have a sign, just a flickering neon cocktail glass hanging in the window.

What was I doing walking into that dark smoke filled bar? So many old guys sat around playing checkers or dozing over their one beer quota that I had trouble spying my old guy.

After standing in the middle of the room long enough to become an object of interest I found him just sitting down at table by the window. I hurried over to him, anxious to be out of there. I placed the knife on the table in front of him and gestured back toward the street.

He grabbed the knife and stood up. His rummy eyes watered fiercely, but who knew the reason. Old age or cold or emotion. He grabbed me in a feeble bear hug and kissed me on both cheeks. I told him you're welcome and fled back to the street.

Stew on the Menu

It was early April of 1992 and we were in Moscow for a math meeting. The conference was held at a university on the very south edge of the city and our accommodations were nearby. We were at least ten blocks from the last stop on the metro. The view from our window was birch trees and dry grass for as far as we could see.

The hotel, if it was, indeed, a hotel, had a restaurant and a gift shop. The gift shop sold mainly hard liquor, postcards, and tee shirts. Lucky for me they also sold Pringles potato chips.

The restaurant was magnificent. Velvet curtains, a hundred or more small round tables with brocade covers, crystal and gold chandeliers—the works.

We were the only patrons that first night, but then it was early. A lady in a long dress and too much lipstick led us to a table, handed us huge menus with leather covers, then disappeared. The menu was in several languages and described the usual chorus of choices. After a few minutes of reading we closed the menu to indicate we were ready.

Two waiters appeared. They wore decidedly shabby tuxes with white shirts and bow ties. Each had a folded towel over one forearm. They bowed, then stood at attention.

We indicated our choices on the menu and were answered with a negative shake of the heads and 'Sorry.' We worked our way through the entire menu in that fashion, then thumped the useless thing closed.

'What, then?' we asked.

'We bring,' said the younger waiter and the two of them disappeared into the kitchen.

They reappeared a few minutes later with two steaming bowls. Each had a browned crust of dough over the bowl and down the sides and steam vented through a series of artistic cuts in the surface. A very large silver spoon came along. The waiters gathered up the rest of the cutlery on the table and wished us 'Bon Appetite.'

Under the crust was a thick stew with lumps of meat, carrots, potatoes, and other unidentified vegetables. Turnips? Parsnips? The meat was strong, but chewable. We tried to figure out what beast we were eating, but came to no conclusion.

When the waiter reappeared, we forked out a morsel and asked him what it was. He appeared puzzled, then summoned the other waiter. Then the cook appeared. He was a greasy fellow in a smeared t-shirt and long apron. He squinted at the meat, then let out a roar and did an unmistakable impression of a bear, raking the air with outstretched hands and lumbering around the room.

Bear stew and it was the only menu item for the duration of our stay. Bear stew and potato chips.

Hotel Ukraina

The Hotel Ukraina in Moscow. One of the 'seven sisters' commissioned by Joseph Stalin, designed by Arkady Mordvinov and Vyacheslav Oltarzhevsky and opened for business on May 25, 1957. [My spell checker just slapped me up side the head.]

Standing in the circle drive at the entrance facing the 650 foot tall hotel, one of the seven 'birthday cake' sky scrapers in Moscow, the first ring road and the Moskva River are behind us along with the 'White House' of the Russian Parliament and Novy Arbat Street leading to the Kremlin. It is August 13, 1994.

We had spent the past four days in St. Petersburg, then rode the day train to Moscow where we were met by friends and driven to the hotel. Not the hotel we had reserved though. On an earlier visit we had stayed at the Rossiya Hotel across from Red Square. It was close to everything. Quiet and nearly deserted. It was also the home of more cockroaches than I had ever seen and I had seen several million living in Southern Illinois.

Hard to tell at first glance, but the Hotel Ukraina would prove to be infested with a different species of cockroaches. The human variety.

The parking area was filled with black cars and their drivers who would have made good characters in a movie about Chicago mob activities. Inside, dark skinned men in suits and speaking Arabic littered every chair, couch, and bench in the lobby. The check-in clerk muttered something about them waiting for the casino to open.

He took our passports and visas, then gave us a room key and pointed to the elevators. Six high speed elevators to connect all thirty stories of the building, he said. Was that meant to be reassuring or to instill fear? We picked up our backpacks and headed through the mob scene.

Our rooms were in one of the corner towers on about the 28th or 29th floor. The first room was highly unsuitable because the water in the bathroom would not shut off. After an argument with the floor lady we were moved to a corner room whose biggest flaw was getting the door open. Not a bad problem compared to non-stop water flow and easily solved by getting the floor lady to open it up each time we returned to the room.

The view from that corner room was spectacular. Big windows revealed a major portion of the city clear to the skyline. The Russian White House across the river, the inner circle with St. Basil's and the Kremlin a short distance beyond. The rackety elevator, congested lobby, peeling paint, drippy faucets all forgotten.

My first up close and personal encounter with the hotel riff-raff and magnificent hotel staff occurred the next morning. I went downstairs to change some money. As much as the Russians wanted hard currency, certain transactions had to be, by law, in rubles.

Off the lobby one person was working the money change booth. And about fifty rumpled suit wearing men were lined up to change money. Pushing and shouting, they tried to speed up the line. The gambling tables were waiting.

I figured I had a long wait ahead of me and took a place at the tail of the line. The coat check lady noticed me and we exchanged silent greetings. No point wasting words when we had no common language. She watched the mob scene at the change money place for about thirty seconds, then took action.

Grabbing a nearby broom, she headed for the biggest, loudest gambler and took a swing. Shrieking and swinging she worked her way through the mob and soon had them backed against the wall.

Then she lowered her broom, took me by the arm and led me to the cashier's window. The gamblers meekly and quietly lined up behind me. The following morning all she had to do to clear the way was point a finger at them when I appeared in the doorway.

Breakfast at the Hotel Ukraina

While we were preparing to fly to Moscow for a meeting, everyone had advice for us. Take your own penicillium and lots of granola bars. A phrase book and language tapes. The phone number of the US Embassy. Was there a US Embassy? Never trust the cab drivers, take extra warm clothes. In August? Are you kidding. Extra shoes. The streets and sidewalks are rough. Nonsense, that's true of the entire world including my home turf.

From the long lists of helpful hints I selected one. Take lots of money. In small bills. A whole bag of one dollar bills. Bulkier than my entire wardrobe, camera, and toiletries. The bag was empty by the time we flew back to Amsterdam, but the visit had been virtually bump free.

The Hotel Ukraina was a huge place with more than 550 rooms. One large open space on the ground floor was used for the breakfast service. Loads of food from many cultures was spread out on tables at one end of the room. Pickled stuff and rice for those from the Orient, eye watering curries, Greek lamb, tacos, and chili. Tacos for breakfast in Russia? America was represented by scrambled eggs and a dry breakfast cereal that vaguely resembled corn flakes.

All of it was self service except for coffee, tea, and juice. One stooped, gray-haired lady pushed a cart among the tables serving drinks. With my breakfast plate in front of me, I watched her progress and decided she would not make it to our table before lunch time. The mob of tourists and businessmen were all taking their own sweet time sorting through the drink selections and arguing with the besieged server. I got up and made my way over to her

I smiled, indicated that I wanted coffee, then handed her two one dollar bills. She decided I was the only person in the room and followed me back to my table. She served coffee all around, stuffed the money into her dress front, then went back to serving the endless crowd.

The next morning she spotted me first and hurried to our table. Dollar bills went her way, coffee mine. We were both happy campers for the entire seven days we stayed at the Ukraina. On the last morning I gave her ten dollars and bid her goodbye. In return I got a good hug and a kiss on both cheeks. A fair exchange.

Ladies Calling

Our first evening at the Hotel Ukraina we had several odd phone calls. The connection was noisy and static drowned out the caller. About all that could be made out was something that sounded like 'Russian six.' Not expecting any calls, we chalked it up to wrong numbers and an antique phone system.

The following evening and the next it happened again with the distinct feminine voice repeating the same phrase. When I asked other Americans staying at the hotel they said that they, too, were getting the same calls. They thought the callers might be saying 'Russian sex.'

On the evening of the fourth day I took the rickety elevator to the lobby. I had previously avoided that perilous journey in the evening because the elevator stopped at every floor until it was jammed past full. When it finally thumped to a stop in the lobby, we untangled ourselves and stepped out. An actually step down because the elevator never quite managed to match up with the floor.

I walked to the lobby phone bank just behind the breakfast room. A dozen or more pay phones lined the wall. And a whole cadre of scantily dressed ladies waited their turn to begin their evening work. Each had a list of room numbers and a purse full of phone friendly coins. The first one I saw hit the jackpot, quickly marked her list, and walked over to a man standing in the shadows.

I had not noticed him before, but he looked like the poster boy for pimps. Big in all directions, slick suit with sagging trousers, well chewed cigar, and needing a shave. He copied the number of the potential customer from the girl's list into his notebook, then patted her on the butt to send her off to work. It wasn't 'Russian six,' it was 'Russian sex.'

Buying Saint George

The Arbat shopping street just inside the first ring road in Moscow was almost bare of outside vendors. In other years they had crowded the sidewalks and spilled into the street. They offered a strange array of items. Watches, pens, souvenir buttons, cigarettes by the smoke [matches extra], knit shawls, embroidered table clothes, even puppies kept in the sellers coat for warmth.

As I waited for a coffee shop to open, I watched delivery trucks and vans move cautiously up and down the pedestrian only stretch of the old 15th Century trade route. When the deliveries were complete and the street empty and quiet again, an ancient Trabant car pulled up. Three ladies got out and began unloading display stands and boxes of handiwork. They were babushka wearing women with worn ankle wrenching shoes, and gray coats that barely fastened in front.

While they labored, a spritely girl arrived in a taxi. She had a large portfolio and a folding display rack. As she set up her work near where I stood, she explained that she was an art student at Moscow University.

The blond haired girl's offerings were mainly silk screen wall hangings and banners. Their bright colors contrasted with the more conservative wares of the ladies across the way. The trio had tables loaded with embroidered table cloths, knit caps, scarves, and gloves, all tones of brown and off white.

Even though the coffee shop behind us had opened, I lingered to look through the wall hangings. Between blue and white scenes of birch trees in winter I found a large picture in red and gold of Saint George. George bore large wings and the dragon had transformed into a cringing Satan. It was the martyred George continuing to fight evil.

W agreed on a price of $20 in US money and the girl removed the hanging from the rack to fold it into a book sized square. Sirens and screeching tires interrupted.

A small police van roared into view from a side street. It crossed the Arbat, jumped the curb, and stopped an inch or so from the table loaded with handwork. Two uniformed policemen jumped out and began hauling the three women's items into the van. When even the tables were swept up, the women were handcuffed and forced into the van.

As I stood staring at this display of police activity, the artist girl grabbed my arm. Go, she said. Into the coffee shop. I'll take care of this. I tell them this is exhibit. All legal.

From the café window I watched her walk out and meet the policemen in the middle of the street. She gestured a welcome to them. An invitation to view her art.

The younger officer fingered through her silk screened banners, while his partner checked her ID papers. They kicked at her display easel, then wrote out something on their ticket pad and handed the girl a copy. As they drove off, she gave me the all clear and began straightening up her banners.

That looked rough I said. What will happen to the women?

They will be back tomorrow. Not to worry.

Why not you? I asked.

No prices, all different. Not like pile of doilies or napkins.

I gave her the twenty dollar bill and dropped St. George into my bag.

COLD WATER

Brussels 2001

We stepped off the train from Aachen into the crowded streets of Brussels with no idea of where to go. A nice lady gestured us to a side street that looked like an alley and held up three fingers. We took that as directions and headed through the crowd.

Sure enough, three long blocks later we came out at the end of the main square of the old town. Two hotels awaited our choice. We settled on the one without a tour bus unloading passengers. We dumped our meager belongings in our room, cleaned up a bit, then headed out to explore.

Chocolate and lace—those are the big selling points of tourist Brussels. A huge market building nearby had an over flow of both items. Alas, the chocolate was far inferior to a good snickers bar and the lace looked like mail order kitchen curtains. I passed on both.

On the other end of the square we found an ancient building labeled 'town hall' or something like that. The Gothic building was pretty interesting with many bits of history displayed. We spent the rest of the afternoon walking the streets and then, looking for a good, cheap place to eat.

Next morning we got up at our usual 5 o'clock to discover there was no hot water. Two very cold showers later we went down to breakfast. By then there was no water at all and the neighboring hotel was being evacuated. Sleepy tourists wearing bathrobes or blankets milled around in the street while firemen and a city crew splashed around hunting a water main break.

The tour group was still shivering in the street when we paid our bill, grabbed our stuff, and headed for the train station. So much for Brussels.

And Again

Cold Water at Schiphol

Rotterdam, the last stop on our month long journey from Cluj, Romania, proved to be an interesting place, but it was definitely time to head home. The huge backlog of flights canceled by 9-11 had finally thinned out and there seemed be some chance that we could fly home on October 1 as scheduled.

Almost. The smiling girl at the KLM counter said sorry, we'll re-book you for tomorrow. In the mean time there is a bus waiting at station four. It will take you to our hotel. A one day wait—not bad.

The KLM hotel was a bare bones affair on the very edge of Amsterdam. Its cement block construction was evident and the rooms clustered around the central dining area were small. However, that dining room made delayed travelers forget their troubles. It was a continuous 24 hour buffet of breakfast, lunch and dinner. Masses of very excellent dishes prepared by trained chefs reached out to weary, frustrated travelers.

We ate and rested, ate and had a walk around the neighborhood, then ate some more. It was one of the more entertaining days of our entire trip. Who knew a cement block building in the suburbs could be more enticing than art museums and cathedrals. Cheap too. The airline footed the entire thing. Room, board, and transportation. Lock, stock, and barrel.

The only glitch showed up the next morning. No hot water. The sheer volume of travelers had drained the supply. Unwilling to face a trans Atlantic flight unwashed, I sucked it up and had the coldest shower ever. Breakfast soothed the memory and we were soon back at the airport for our flight home.

When Security is not Secure

After a totally splendid week in Istanbul we settled our bill at the Best Western and requested a driver to the airport.

From our location just outside the walls of the old city we were driven along the waterfront, then through busy city streets to the airport. The revolving doors at the airport revealed a pretty bare bones facility with a sterile security check just inside the front door. From there we were directed upstairs.

Our flight to Bucharest was several hours away so we had time to eat, walk the hallways, and look through the shops for last minute bits of junk. On what seemed like my billionth trip around the departure floor I noticed another set of escalators from the far end of the entrance floor.

After watching people come and go up this set of escalators I decided to try it myself. Down I went. Now on the ground floor, I exited the building via a set of revolving doors and found myself in the parking lot. Swell. Now to go back in. There must be a trick to this someplace.

Back in through the revolving doors. No problem. Up the escalator and Bingo! I'm back in the secure portion of the airport. So much for keeping the bad guys out.

And why did the bad guys attack the security area of the airport a few years later, when they could have had access using the parking lot entrance?

148

The Long Journey Into Romania

It was September of 2001 that we flew into Budapest to begin our journey to Cluj-Napoca, Romania. We spent the night at the Hungaria Grand Hotel where the food was great and the rooms just so, so. The next morning we took a taxi to Nugati Station to board the train.

It was one of the old Soviet era trains we had used so often when we lived in Hungary in 1985. Noisy, slow, and unkempt. This one looked like it had seen no maintenance or cleaning in all those years. Sixteen or seventeen years of neglect for sure. Probably much more.

Three cars long, it had been billed as an express train. But then it was the only train, so they could call it anything they wanted. Nine hours of boring misery would have nailed it.

We did have a compartment to ourselves. Actually we had the whole first class car to ourselves. Everyone else was jammed into the two second class cars. A very stern train official kept us separated. Too bad. The woman with a crate of chickens would have been entertaining.

We had bought food and bottled water in the station so the train's lack of either didn't bother us. The crusted stink of the bathroom was another matter. They had hosed it down from ceiling to floor in the station, but that had little effect on the filth of eons. Mostly the hose down made everything drippy and slimy.

We settled into the creaky red leather seats and waited for the last passengers to ascend the steep steps and arrange their baggage. The train slid out of the station exactly on time.

Budapest to the edge of Romania was flat and nearly treeless. Huge tracts of land that had once been collective farms.

The farther east we went, the more primitive the farms and small towns appeared. Horse drawn wagons waited at the railroad crossings and family milk cows were staked out in the small pastures near thatched roof houses. Men and women alike worked in the fields with long handled scythes cutting and stacking hay for winter. Each house had an old fashioned well with a dip handle and an outhouse. The houses along the rail line did have electricity, but not running water or indoor plumbing. Each one was a scene from an old painting.

Except for one thing. Television had come to rural Hungary and Romania. Every single farm house we passed had a satellite dish. Some dishes sat on metal stands near the house or fastened to a fence. Others were balanced on the thatch of the roof and secured with guy wires. Apparently the sod walls of the houses were not good supports for the antennas.

What were these hard working people watching after a grueling day? Old episodes of Baywatch or Friends? Subtitled clips from Monday Night Football or the X-Files? It must make getting up at the crack of dawn very difficult or maybe they just slept through Dan Rather giving the news in a language few understood. So much for the accoutrements of the modern world.

At the border the train stopped and Hungarian officials came on to stamp our passports. We could see a long line of abandoned guard towers marking the edge of Hungary. A no man's land followed before we entered Romania. We pulled into a village where customs officials came on to provide us with exit/entry permits.

An hour later we reached our destination, the city of Cluj.

Some Beds I Have Known And Bedrooms Too

Who knew you could write a story with beds as the main character. Some babies start life in a bassinet, a dresser drawer, a cardboard box, or snuggled between doting parents. Others scream non-stop and spend most of their early months being jiggled in some harried adult's arms. Fortunately we don't remember that part of our history.

The Old Crib

What I do know about is the old crib that bedded me and my brothers over the years. The crib was old when my mother bought it at a second hand store in 1941. War year shortages left most stores bereft of such items and she was more than put out when she had to haul the old crib home for her first born.

Intense scrubbing and a new mattress cover helped her peace of mind. The drop front crib wouldn't pass any safety inspections today, but it served us well. None of us ever poked our heads through the wide spaced bars or slipped between the mattress and the back panel. We shook it and kicked it, slobbered and pooped all over it. Still it stood.

My dad moved the crib from our house in Lead, South Dakota to my grandmother's house in Spearfish when he went off to work on the fuel tank rebuild in Honolulu. He moved it again when he returned a year later. In fact he folded it up and forced it into the trunk of our old Chevy three more times that year. When I was done with it, it ended up in my grandma's cellar.

When each of my brothers were born, the crib was bumped up the crooked steps of my grandmother's cellar and hauled home where it was scrubbed and re-varnished. When we moved from South Dakota to Washington, the crib came too, lashed to the top of our trailer along with the bikes.

At our new home in Pasco the crib was stowed in the rafters of the garage forever after. It may still be there.

The Grain Elevator

There were a few other beds before the Roundup Cabin Camp, but they were only for short intervals. A cot in the attic of an old farmhouse in Albany, Missouri while my dad went to school on the GI bill, a scratchy couch at an uncle's house, a shared bed at my grandmother's house.

When my dad finished his courses, we moved to Belle Fourche to search for a house. Nothing was available. We signed a nine month lease with the owner of the Roundup Cabin Camp. The cabins were old grain elevators hauled in from the prairie and remodeled.

Ours had sleeping space on the second floor right under the rafters with room for a mattress and the crib. We all, parents and two kids, slept jammed in there. No floor space. If you hung your head over the edge of the mattress, you were peering straight down the steep stairs. Pretty cozy.

Army Surplus Bunks at the Day Street House

When we finally found a house in Belle Fourche, it was totally bereft of furniture. We had a couple of weeks before our lease at the Roundup Cabins was up, so we scurried around like a batch of berserk chipmunks looking for beds and chairs and the like. Lack of money limited our shopping options to second hand stores and the Army surplus store in Sturgis.

It was the surplus store that solved the problem of beds for me and my brother. My dad carted home an Army green set of bunk beds. Neither of us could stand the thought of sleeping in an upper bunk, so my dad cut down the legs and the excess posts, then painted the newly created twin beds white. He ran out of paint before he could apply a second coat to my bunk so it remained a bit grayish green all the years we lived there.

The bunks were considerably narrower than a standard twin bed and had a thin mattress on a wire mesh stretched over the frame. It would have been an uncomfortable mess for an adult, but me and my brother thought it was a great improvement over sleeping on the improvised plywood floor of a grain elevator.

The house had interior walls with a certain amount of insulation too. It had required a huge mound of quilts to stay warm in the drafty grain elevator. And we had floor space and a dresser. No door and an annoying smell of gas from the meter outside the window didn't seem to bother us.

The old crib was set up in our parents' bedroom for our new little brother. Not much floor space in that room.

I slept in that bunk through the end of 7th grade. I think I had permanent bruises on the side of my head from hitting the bed rails every time I turned over, but luxury awaited when we moved to Washington.

A Headboard Even

After sleeping on the couch in my aunt's living room for two months we finally found a house. A brand new, just built house with three bedrooms. We found a cut rate furniture place that advertised whole rooms of furniture, lamps, end tables, and pictures included and soon had a cozy place to live.

The very first thing we bought even before the whole room packages was a TV set. There had been no TV in our part of South Dakota and this was the greatest thing since sliced bread.

I had a bedroom to myself. With a three quarter size bed with a headboard where I could stow books, a clock, and a few ceramic horses. One downside to a bed of such an odd size was that I never had new sheets. My always saving mother would split the old worn through sheets down the middle and sew the outside edges together to make a new sheet somewhat smaller than the original and the perfect size for my bed.

Except for sharing my bed with a drunken aunt who came to visit a few times a year, I had that snug room to myself all through Middle School, High School, and a year at a local college. Then I got married and the bed train picked up speed. I had ten years and a dozen different beds to my credit by that time.

An Old Pull Down

Married beds started with a dingy spring broke double in a tiny apartment in Pasco, then moved to a basement apartment in an ancient campus building between the two gymnasiums in Pullman, Washington home of the Cougars. It was a one room apartment with a pull down bed that filled most of the space. Murphy beds I think they called them.

College Court was cheap and in walking distance of most of the campus. For sixty dollars a month, utilities included, it served us well and saved us big bucks.

We did have one intermission when we drove to Los Angeles where my husband had a summer job on the moon landing project. The apartment was nondescript, but the building inhabitants were not. Every morning we awoke to a chorus of coughing up and down the building. The LA cough. By the time we left to go back to school, we were coughing too.

Our last semester at WSU we were forced out of our cozy basement and had several different places to our credit before we graduated and moved to Canada. Those beds were old, worn, and lumpy.

A House and a Floor

In Edmonton we found a house to rent. A house with zero furniture. We did have a bit more money though. A couch and chair and the cheapest chrome leg dinette set soon graced our new happy home. Beds were another matter. For some reason they were pricey and did not include the usual frame and/or legs. We ended up sleeping on a new mattress on the floor. No pillows either. Back ache city was my opinion.

The Pineapple Bed

We survived two years in the province of Alberta before we headed south to the tail end of Illinois. Beds were pretty nondescript for the next few years. Then we found a splendid piece in an antique/junk store in a nearby town. It was a hundred year old pineapple bed frame. The mahogany affair had tall posts with carved tops. Our Canadian mattress fit, but just barely.

It was a good step up to get into the new bed and a fine thump if you should fall out, but we got used to it quickly. The posts soon became hangers for shirts and jeans, but the solid headboard kept the cold draft from the front door away from my head.

As the years passed the need of a new bed became more and more obvious. We bought a pair of twin beds and advertised the pineapple bed frame for sale. Two ladies from a nearby town decided to love it and paid us what we had laid out twenty years before.

In the era of the pineapple bed we often ventured to other territories and other beds. Aluminum frame camp cots and a cheap tent got us from Southern Illinois to the Washington coast a number of summers. At the beach we had an old trailer house that had served a sheep herder for years. The bed was a platform across the tiny cave-like back room of the trailer with a beat up mattress and barely enough room to turn over.

But the cheap tent got shaky with age and hard use. It blew down on us in a wind storm in Montana. We got used to tying it to the car top carrier's rails to steady it in windy places. A few times we had to abandon the idea of sleeping in the great outdoors, pulled up stakes, literally, and headed to a motel. One time I heard growling and snuffling in the middle of the night, peered out the door flap and found myself face to face with a big bear. I finished the night sleeping in the car. Camping was getting tiresome.

Expanding Our Bed History

In 1985 we went to Hungary for the fall semester. A whole new era of beds opened up. Our apartment was quite nice for that Soviet controlled era. It belonged to a professor on sabbatical elsewhere. A large living room and bathroom along with a small kitchen, a very small bedroom with a child size bunk, a room of unknown use, and a room that appeared to be a library made up the corner third floor walk up apartment. When we asked about our sleeping place, the guide flipped a panel in the 'library' and reached up to pull down a clone of our old college days, a Murphy bed. We were to sleep surrounded by miles of books written in Hungarian.

As the weeks unfolded we became infinitely more appreciative of our apartment. The similar apartment in the other corner of the building was inhabited by at least three families and in two cases three generations of those families. An almost uncountable number of people jammed into an apartment the same size as ours. They worked and slept in shifts. The old grandfathers were put out on the balcony without their pants and shoes [to keep them from running off to the tavern down the block] to get them out of the way of cleaning and cooking.

Home Again, But Not For Long

Spain

We were home for just one semester when we headed for a summer in Madrid. There it wasn't the beds that were so memorable, but rather the noise at night. Our first apartment in a high rise in the north part of the city was in the hospital district which was also near the university. It was comfortable enough except for the non-stop sirens.

It seemed like every car accident, every precarious birth, every shooting and stabbing happened after dark and required screaming sirens and ambulance trips through the ever present traffic, over curbs, down narrow sidewalks and over pedestrian bridges to the appropriate medical facility. It made sleeping a crap shoot.

After a month of that mayhem we moved to a downtown apartment a block above the Prado Art Museum. It seemed like a quiet neighborhood that shut down after hours. The first morning I was awakened by a great clashing and clanging. It was 3am. I went out on the balcony to see what was going on. On the street below was a rickety wagon with two sleepy horses. The junk pickers had arrived. We would probably call them recyclers today, but then they were scavengers hunting through the trash left at the curb.

They searched every metal can with great flourishes, often bashing the lids together like cymbals and yelling to one another when some treasure appeared.

There was trash pickup nearly every morning in that district because of the many small shops and eateries, but the noise really escalated when a long steel construction waste collector was hauled to the curb down the street. An apartment was being renovated and all of its interior discarded.

First on the scene to sort through the mess was a rough old fellow with a cart made of welded pipe with two car tires and a cantankerous mule to provide the go power. His glee at finding such a treasure trove was unmistakable and he was first on the scene every morning at daybreak.

We weren't much good at sleeping in anyway and took up the Spanish habit of the afternoon nap to keep us going.

Finnish Luxury

We had been to a meeting in St. Petersburg, Russia and decided to look around Finland for a few days. The train ride from St. Petersburg to Helsinki was easy and scenic. Another train took us to Turku on the west side of the Finnish land mass. Though it was summer, a harsh cold wind blew through the city. I had made reservations at the only hotel I could find on line, but when we arrived at the place it was bursting with guests.

The desk clerk found our reservation, but seemed to think the hotel was full up and over-booked. He hurried off to find his manager. I watched their earnest conversation in the glass cubicle across the lobby. When the clerk returned, he was visibly happier. I was even happier when he said not to worry. We have a room for you. Same price. Patrice will take you.

We followed the spiffy lady in the tight skirt and very high heels across the lobby to the elevator. The princess leading the beggars. What awaited us? A broom closet? Or the smallest room known to man?

The elevator stopped at the top floor which was totally quiet. The thick carpet drowned out our footfalls as we followed her to the end of the hall. She unlocked a door and handed us the key. Call if you need anything, she said and disappeared back to the elevator.

The room turned out to be bigger than most apartments. To the left was a dining room or conference room with a long

polished table, coffee maker, and a spectacular view of the river. The bedroom filled the other end of the apartment.
The center piece was the bathroom. It had glass floor to ceiling walls. A panoramic view of the city vied with a very red bathtub front and center in full view of anyone in the apartment.

A huge sauna all fired up and ready connected to the bathroom. Fired up for some other guest? A very important one no doubt. Not us disheveled travelers.

The floor to ceiling windows continued into the bedroom and provided a view of the night sky as well as the city. The view vied with the flat screen TV on the wall at the foot of the bed for the sleeper's attention. The bed itself was huge with a ton of pillows and comforters. The bed with its promise of deep, dreamless sleep won that tug of war.

Turku proved to be an interesting town though I may have been looking at it through the rosy glow of our luxury hotel. We explored the old town and the churches, ate at an excellent Italian Restaurant, and suffered with the fierce cold wind that marred the summer day. We decided to spend another night. The desk clerk told us he would move us to a regular room, but then decided to leave us where we were. Two dips in the red bathtub before we hit the trail again.

Old Florence

One fall we went to Florence, Italy for a month or so. Our host found us an apartment in a 'palace' near the center of town. Built by an Englishman in 1870, the palace part was the second floor where the owner lived. Our part was the converted stables and scullery. Twenty foot ceilings and stained glass did little to mitigate the tiny rooms and lack of hot water in the kitchen. The two very small bedrooms opened onto a walled garden at the back of the palace.

My room was long and very narrow with a small platform bed built across the back of the room. The astounding feature was the frescoed walls and ceiling. A Japanese scene with white birds and branches of cherry blossoms decorated three walls and the twenty foot ceiling. At least down to the nine foot level where the whole thing became a flakey, faded mess.

The flood of 1966, commented our landlady. The Arno River covered this entire neighborhood.

I was to sleep in a bed that had had nine foot of flood waters over it once upon a time not so long ago. It was also a very cold bed even though I spread my coat and rain coat on top of the scant covers at night. Thinking about nine foot of flood water along with the cold should have given me trouble sleeping, but I wasn't much good at that. If I woke up drowned, then so be it.

I became very aware of the fall rains that pounded down every few days. Especially at night. Soon I discovered I was not the only one that worried.

After a few weeks of exploring the city I added a daily trek to the banks of the Arno to my schedule. Me and a growing crowd of onlookers. We watched the river rise higher around the piers of the bridge. After a week or so water was smacking against the concrete retaining wall by the path. Debris swirled in the water and piled up around the bridge piers.

Late in our stay I found the water lapping over the river walk. Paired with a couple of days of hard rain worry spread. Police with their caped rain coats patrolled the river bank and new barricades kept us from our usual viewing place. My husband and I decided to head for home a few days early. We packed our few belongings and got the train for Venice and the airport. The newspaper the next day reported widespread flooding in Florence.

An Italian Dinner

We had been in Florence several weeks when we were invited to dinner at the apartment of a well known mathematician. It was a Friday in the middle of October. We were picked up at 8:00pm for the 9:00 O'clock meal. That was our normal bedtime so we took naps in the afternoon to stay awake later. We would make pretty crappy Italians.

The meal, the supposed high point of the visit, was served some time well after nine. We started out with thin bread spread with cream cheese and some gummy stuff which turned out to be chopped up mushrooms.

Not just any old mushrooms though. They were a species of boletus, rare as hen's teeth. Being somewhat versed in fungus identification, I poked around in my portion to be sure there were no red spots which would identify it as a poisonous bolete mushroom called Satan's Cap. No red, so I ate the concoction.

The next course was pastry cups with a cream and pea filling served hot. Not too bad. Peas are edible. The pastry cups were followed by a big pasta filled with cottage cheese, olive oil, and sage.

Thin slices of beef over a pulp of beet greens and spinach topped off the main course. The Italians must have learned cooking from the Spanish because each item was served separately. A long way from our tradition of putting everything out at once so the eater could mix things together or keep them separate as they pleased.

Dessert was a flan with almond flavored caramel, then grapes and coffee, small and strong. Grapes and coffee. Good grief. The flan would have matched better.

After supper we had entertainment. Not dancing girls or musicians, but a display of very old treasures. One of the ladies had an Egyptian scarab set into a necklace. It was as splendid as anything in a museum. Our host had an Etruscan bowl and two very fine unglazed jugs from about 2000 BC. These items were handed around for our inspection.

After supper conversation included the mushrooms we had eaten. 'The Boletes are very expensive,' Our host explained. 'They are wild, not cultivated. And highly protected by the government.' 'Why are we eating them,' I wanted to ask, but didn't.

Politics was the next topic—the presidential debates and the American press—they didn't really understand it, but then does anyone? They did seem to think the debates were very important.

The conversation turned to the weather and possible flooding of the Arno River and went downhill from there.

Somewhere about midnight the party broke up and someone drove us back to our apartment. It was an interesting outing, but no way to live.

Around the World 1990

In late spring we were informed that my husband had been awarded a Senior Fulbright Fellowship to Hungary. We had had a similar opportunity in 1985 and found it to be a marvelous experience.

After a trip to Washington D.C. for orientation meetings we began making plans for the journey. We had a previous commitment in Japan so we were going to Budapest the wrong way around the world.

We managed to get a special airline ticket for 'around the world.' One price for as much travel as we could manage as long as we didn't back track more than once. It cost about $1000.

In August the journey began. We closed down the homestead—cleaning, shutting off, unplugging, stowing, and throwing out the remaining perishables in the fridge. Our very good neighbors across the road agreed to tend the animals, bring in the mail and newspapers, and mow the lawn. For a price of course.

We bummed a ride into town with another friend and caught the transport to St. Louis. We were off.

We flew to Seattle via Minneapolis and stayed three cold nights with my brother and his wife in West Seattle. We left Seattle and flew to Narita airport in Japan. From Narita we flew to Osaka, then took the train to Kyoto where we stayed at the U and I Hotel across from the royal palace grounds. My husband attended his meetings, gave his lecture and I went sightseeing.

It was September before we flew from Japan, across The Soviet Union to Amsterdam. One of the first commercial flights on that route in years.

We had four full days to explore Amsterdam. We went through the Ann Frank house, visited the Old and New Churches, and the main square with its mess of pigeons. Another day we had a boat ride through the canals and out into the harbor. The third day we toured the countryside and visited a cheese farm with goats and a wooden house village.

The next stop was Vienna. From Vienna we traveled to Budapest, Hungary where we stayed the night at a favorite hotel, the Forum, on the bank of the Danube. That was the end of 'normal' for awhile. It was September 13, 1990. We were just a few short weeks from public mayhem.

On the 14th we got a taxi to the metro station across the river to buy subway passes and move to our apartment which was on the castle side of the Danube. The first indication of trouble reared its head as we approached the station. About fifty taxi drivers were circling the block, honking and leaning out their windows to shake their fist and scream undecipherable complaints at anyone who dared to cross their line.

Our driver shrugged it off as he maneuvered through the line to the drop off lane. He indicated it was something to do with the price of gas, but his English was not up to the politics of the situation.

We bought our passes and found another working taxi to haul us up Goat Hill to our new apartment. It was a long way from anything. Located on the second street from the top of a very steep hill, it overlooked a wooded valley. Even the goats would have complained. There was a small grocery store and a bus stop about a block down the hill from us. It was a precarious walk to a store with little to offer. The University and the city were miles away.

I wrote in my notebook: "It seems like several centuries have passed. We have been in Budapest nearly a week now. It has been a very hard week putting together an existence here. Much has changed, but much more remains the same. Decent food with any variety is still not available. Ditto cleaning products and paper products. No peanut butter either. A great array of exotic sauces and noodles from China, but few vegetables fresh or canned. The grocery store is still perfumed with the stink of unrefrigerated meat.

Electronic stuff of every sort is available as well as rock music and hip clothing. Noise, pollution, pornography, crime, and greed smear this once pristine city. The worst of the West has arrived."

People wanted the newly available Western goods, but didn't have the salary to match the wants. Many had 2nd and 3rd jobs. Others sold booze and guns on the black market. Long lines of people stood or sat on the sidewalks at the metro stops selling flowers, produce, craftwork, family heirlooms, used clothing, and junk.

Of course not all of them were selling so they could buy TV's and VCRs or a long dreamed of car. Many were the newly poor whose incomes could not cover the inflation that came with the attempt to change to a market economy. There was a whole new class of people here. The unemployed. It grew daily, fed by the influx of refugees and more and more people who lost their guaranteed jobs in the Communist system.

In spite of the protests transportation continued. We seemed to spend about half of our time riding trains to somewhere and back or riding city transit. The rest of the time we spent shopping and washing clothes. The protests continued, but the police mostly kept it contained.

We had no trouble finding places in Budapest to visit. It is a city of museums. Most were empty of visitors that fall.

Our trips away from our apartment on Goat Hill also revealed our total isolation from the city itself. Yes, we had less air pollution and maybe huffing up that block from the bus stop was good for us, but it grew boring and we were looking forward to moving to the city of Szeged when our two months in Budapest were complete.

In October three days honoring Hungary's 1956 uprising against Soviet occupation turned into a tool for the union of taxi drivers. The 1956 uprising failed and plunged the country into 35 more years of Soviet control. In 1989 Hungary again flung off the tentacles of Soviet domination. The Soviets did not take this well and the Hungarians were ill prepared to deal with the practical side of independence.

The lasting blow was the price of oil. For years Hungary had enjoyed cheap oil, and its companion cheap gasoline, from Russia. Because of the unrest in Budapest, Moscow shut down the pipe lines carrying oil from the USSR to Hungary. The government was forced to buy oil on the free market at much higher prices.

The gasoline reserves were exhausted by the time we arrived in Budapest and in a matter of a few days, the price of gas had gone up nearly 80 percent. The price increase hit the taxi drivers worst of all. They had enjoyed a high ranking on the income scale for years and now they were facing poverty. They were very angry.

The problem escalated as the weeks wore on. Three taxi drivers were murdered the first week we were there. The other drivers held another big protest. Hundreds of them leaning on their horns and tying up rush hour traffic which seemed to last from 8am to 8pm. A huge increase in theft, car snatching, and robbery was also noted in the local paper. Greed and survival went hand in hand.

On October 25, a Thursday, we went to the Museum of Ethnography across from the Parliament, then headed for home on Goat Hill. The Metro was okay, but the bus up the hill was incredibly slow. It stopped short of its usual stop and unloaded all of the passengers. We had a longer than usual trudge home.

There seemed to be masses of cars on the roads. All honking and going every which way. We assumed the traffic lights were on the blink again and didn't worry much about it. When we got home we heard that another gasoline price increase had been announced, but did not connect that with the traffic.

My husband got up very early Friday morning to begin our move to Szeged. He took the backpack and a large sack of our stuff with him. About an hour after he left for Nugatti Station where he was to board the train to Szeged, the radio started talking about the taxi and truck driver strike.

The drivers were using their vehicles to block the bridges across the Danube and all were closed down. By noon the strike had spread to the rest of the country. The price hike on gas had finally sunk in. A nice mess. There was talk of stopping the trains too. I spent the whole day wondering where Ted was and if he made it to Szeged and then, if he'd make it back.

About dark he came home, hardly aware that anything was going on until he thought about it. There had been no taxies in Szeged and no trams going across the bridges in Budapest. On his way back to Budapest the train was stopped by a car placed across the tracks. A group of passengers got off the train and moved the car to the side. The train went on its way, very slowly and eventually arrived in Budapest. Some buses were still in service and he caught one of them for most of the way home on Goat Hill.

By Saturday things were much worse with no buses running on Goat Hill. People were lined up at the stores and there was no bread or milk. By supper time the shelves were empty. Despite the mess, the mood of the crowds of people in the streets was festive. Walkers, bikers, and baby carriages moved from the sidewalks to the roadways. Cheering, singing crowds urged the strikers forward.

There were threats and ultimatums by the strikers. Mobs were trying to close border crossings out of the country. All major highways were blocked. We decided it was time to pack up and take a vacation from Hungary's chaos.

A friend drove us down to Moscow Ter and we found a Metro train to Kelletti Station. We were hoping to get a train to Vienna. The station was mobbed with people with the same idea. People of all sorts with baggage and bundles galore. We were fortunate to get a seat on the train. Second class was packed with people jammed into the aisles and hanging out the windows.

With first class tickets we had a compartment with three other people, an East Indian from Deli who was living in Paris, an Austrian businessman who had to leave his car in Budapest, and a French tourist who slept all the way to Vienna. The Austrian was in the business of arranging the export of fruit juices to the USA. He was calm and spent some time trying to convince the angry man from Deli that Hungarians really were nice people.

When we reached the border, our papers were processed in the usual way, then we sat and waited. Several hours. We watched crowds of strikers try to block the tracks. Others tried to climb onto or into the train. They were rebuffed by railroad employees. The train finally moved out of the station. We were on our way to Vienna.

It was the last train to cross the border that week. The next train was not so lucky. It spent the night there and returned to Budapest the next morning.

We returned a few weeks later when Hungarian life became normal again. We had had a fine vacation in Florence, Italy in the meantime.

Birthday in a Bag

I found this title in my list of story ideas and can't quite figure out what I had in mind when I wrote it. I have scrolled through all the birthdays I can remember and find nothing that would inspire such an idea.

You would think that list of birthdays remembered would be a long one, especially when I decided to include all birthdays rather than zero in on my own. Wrong. The list is pretty skimpy.

The first one I remember happened before I started school. Some kid who lived a couple of blocks over from us. Maybe her mother was a friend or co-worker of my mom. I handed off my wrapped present at the door and joined the dozen or so kids in the living room. The nameless birthday girl wore a frilly dress and there were loads of balloons everywhere.

I felt misplaced with my faded jeans and too small t-shirt. The end of that party couldn't come fast enough. I would be better prepared for the next one.

My mom let me wear the crinkly dress that an aunt had sent me for Christmas to the next party. It was for a neighbor girl named Sherry. We all posed for photos, then ate the bakery cake and smeared its ample frosting on each other. No bags there that I can remember, but I do know that the crinkly dress ended up in the trash.

Then there was my first teen year birthday. I had a cherry pie with crust dyed blue instead of a cake. We sat around the dining room table and blathered on about something. No presents and no bag. It doesn't pay to have a birthday 22 days before Christmas.

Other birthdays did come with presents. Horse figurines in the grade school and junior high days. Glass horses, plastic horses, a pot metal one pretending to be bronze, the herd grew over the years before the tide turned to books and stuffed animals. Books were manageable, the stuffed animals not so much.

The parade of stuffed animals started with a gray mouse. A white goat came along about the time my husband and I moved to the farm. Better than a real goat I guess. A huge green and gold winged dragon followed. The next year it was a stuffed orange tiger at birthday time and a white tiger at Christmas. A spotted leopard and a black panther soon had a monopoly on the living room chairs. Those four foot plush critters take up a lot of room.

A host of smaller creatures came the next few years. Little lions and foxes moved in to keep the big guys company. They were joined by a homemade zebra and a gawky giraffe Some came from the internet, some from craft sales, and others from a local bookstore.

And now I see where the 'bag' came from. Even though we had agreed to a no more humongous stuffed animals policy, I spotted my husband hurrying from the car to a back room with an extra large shopping bag with four legs sticking up out of it. I ignored it.

The creature revealed itself December 3rd. I came home from painting class and opened the bedroom door to be greeted by a stuffed giraffe presiding over the room. Eyeball to eyeball we surveyed each other. My beast in a bag.

Meet Guinevere, your new roommate, said my husband.

The Third Degree Relic

Smack in the middle of my shower I remembered something. Well, almost remembered. A third degree relic. I had a third degree relic of a beloved saint. Relics are bits and pieces left behind by holy people and Jesus, Himself, though these are rare.

Now having a relic is not as exotic as it sounds. Most people think of severed fingers, polished smooth skulls, or an ancient arm bone in a leather case. Nails and splinters from the true cross also abound. Enough splinters are displayed in museums and churches around the world to build a good sized barn. Or as John Calvin noted: "a ship."

The crown of thorns is on display in a dozen or more places. A trio of nuns in a Toledo, Spain church directed me to a glass set in the floor of their building where the baby shoes of Jesus could be viewed. What!! A similar relic is on display in a rural church in Hungary. In any case these things are first and second degree relics.

Third degree relics are the things touched by a saint or touched to something the saint had touched or touched to something touched to something the saint had touched. Get the idea?

Closer degree relics are usually bits of bone, paper, or hair enclosed in a glass container. Third degree relics are almost always tiny pieces of fabric or wood embedded in a drop of red wax, then fixed to the back of a medal. They usually come with a signed certificate written in Latin.

These relics are sold by the fist full at prices determined by the medal itself in shrines and churches around the world. Or, you can fire up your computer and shop for relics on EBay. Prices range from $4.99 to many thousands of dollars. You can buy the cheap ones individually or by the dozen.

Mine is one of the cheap ones. Made of stamped aluminum with a thin neck blackening chain, it features a Madonna and the name of some obscure saint. The back has the dot of red wax with a teeny tiny scrap of course fabric embedded. The name of the saint is stamped in letters so small no one can read them. A bargain at $4.99 postpaid. Now if I can just find it. Or maybe just buy another one. Easier.

Post script: I just found my relic in a box I was preparing to send to Good Will. It wasn't any old saint either, it was Saint George slaying the dragon/devil. And I had two of them just alike. Just in case.

The Doll in the Box

When I cleaned out a closet recently, I found a box my brother had dropped off on a visit a few years back. His drop offs were common and rarely yielded anything of interest. Mostly stuff from our collective childhood that I passed on to the thrift shop.

I stripped off the curling tape and pulled back the card board flaps. A battered doll stared up at me. A big doll from the early 1940's. At first I thought it was a doll my mom and her sister had given me at Christmas the year I turned four.

The doll was dressed in the same red stripe frock my aunt had made and the Swedish costume of white blouse, red vest, and black skirt we had put together for a first grade Christmas display was folded beside her. Still, this battered doll did not look familiar.

Of course she was chipped and broken. Her toes and fingers were worn to the core, one arm barely hanging from the wire that threaded it to her body. Even her painted on eyes and mouth had mostly flaked off. When I undressed her, I knew this doll was an imposter. She had both composition legs attached to her cloth body. My doll had had one composition leg and one of stuffed cloth.

So, what was she doing wearing my doll's clothing. How had she come to be in this box with musty books, my father's Navy sweater, the full length knit stockings we had hung by the chimney with care once a year, and a dismantled music box?

After spending twenty years in the rafters of my mom's garage and another twenty in a stack of similar boxes in my brother's basement there was no answer to the question of how this imposter had squirmed her way into my junk.

    Now, what to do with her. The trash bin seemed an ignoble end, the thrift shop would put some distance between her demise and my silly imaginings. Keep her and consign her to the attic? Re-dress her and find a place for her to look at me with her accusing stare? Bury her in the garden? I didn't even know her name. Why was it harder to deal with someone else's junk than my own? I guess she will just have to live in the box under my studio table until I can stop dithering.

Birds in the Poppies

In the back corner of my yard hard up against a small storage building was a stand of orange poppies. The mass of fronds and tall flowers had grown larger each year until they formed a true thicket.

When the poppies threatened to engulf the nearby rose bushes, I decided to cut them back. They had finished blooming and were now busy making seed pods. A good safe time to wack them into submission.

I had managed to free one rose bush, when something shot up out of the vegetation. I was not alone in the poppy thicket. I decided it was a good time for a coffee break. The poppies could wait for another day.

The next time my cleanup session was even shorter. I never made it to the second rose bush before the poppies exploded with noise and motion and a bird of some sort whirled past me. Someone was living in my thicket.

Over the next few days I made no progress in my quest to free that second rose bush trying to flower under its load of stems and fronds. No matter how carefully I approached, the watch bird caught me. Instead of flying to a nearby apple tree, she started landing on the electric line just above my head.

She seemed to be a thrush of some sort and she was soon joined by her mate. They would sit there and shrill at me until I backed off. I left them in peace for a few days, then returned for another try. The birds now sat on the fence just a few feet away. Their one note shrilling pierced the morning with more urgency than usual.

Before I could cut a single stem a third and then a fourth bird flew up. Their feathers brushed my face as they joined their parents on the fence. Two little brown feathered off spring. No wonder the parent birds had been so protective.

After a few hours of practice the whole family flew off to begin their spring migration to someplace. I turned to clearing out the poppy thicket. Just inside I found the nest and carefully cut it loose from the surrounding stems. It seemed small for two such large fledglings, but then they were pretty puffed up and fluffy when I encountered them.

The tidy little nest now sits in a pottery bowl in my bookcase. Maybe they will be back next year.

The Red Bush

It seems strange that a bush or flower or a tiny plant can evoke memories. The red bush was one such plant. I don't even know its name, but I recognize it instantly.

When we moved to the farm in Southern Illinois, we found the acreage contained the ruins of an old homestead probably dating from the years after the Civil War when the land was deeded to a returning soldier. It was a hilly section of land that grew poison ivy, kudzu, and all manner of weedy crap. But there in the smother of wild vegetation near the ruins of a house, I found the red bush.

That area of our place required a long hike up a steep hill so visiting the red bush didn't happen very often. It actually wasn't red, but it did have a good crop of red flowers that lasted into summer. I decided to try transplanting a piece of it.

A couple of plastic bags, a trowel, and a clipper was about all I was willing to carry up that hill. I snipped some likely shoots and spaded up a smaller bush growing underneath the main one. It was firmly attached to the root of the mama bush and required some effort to remove.

Back at the house I planted the cuttings from the red bush near the foundation and gave them a good soaking. They wilted, turned brown, and seemed doomed. I forgot all about them. A failed experiment.

Come spring they surprised me by greening up with new twigs and shiny leaves. This was followed by a mass of red flowers. They flourished all the rest of the years we lived there. When we decided to move, I hated leaving those faithful friends of thirty years.

We bought a house and settled down in our new town. Once upon a time the place had been professionally landscaped with fancy raised beds, rocks, waterfall, and dozens of overgrown plants and trees. All unfamiliar.

Then, in the spring I discovered a red bush blooming in a nook near the west side of the house. It was the twin of my red bush back in Illinois. I wacked down the neighboring bushes threatening to overwhelm my new friend. I could see that it had suffered more than its share of indignities over the years because it grew next to the entrance for the various wires and pipes that supply a house. Still it looked hopeful. Red bushes are tough customers.

Grandma's Spirea

The only plant I really remember in my grandma's huge garden was the spirea. And the gooseberry bush, but that's another story. She had a whole row of the white flowered bushes forming the barrier on the alley side of the backyard. She also had a few lilacs out front, but they were a feeble lot displaying a few sparse flowers each spring.

The spirea reproduced like mad rabbits until you needed a machete to get to the garbage can. In the spring all sorts of people came by wanting an armful for a wedding or some sort of reception.

When the blooming was over, my uncle pruned the bushes to an inch of their lives and hauled the heap of branches to the dump. And each year my grandma was in despair about the health and welfare of her precious bushes. They always survived and flourished the next spring.

Maybe my attachment to the red bush was an inherited trait.

The Rose of Sharon

The King James version of scripture translates The Song of Solomon 2:1 as "I am the Rose of Sharon, the Lily of the Valley." The idea that the rose is the Christ Child has populated literature, poetry, and music ever since.

It was years before I found out that it was the name of a flower. Sort of like a morning glory in shape, but not really, it couldn't decide if it was a bush, a tree, or a noxious weed. The plant seemed to bloom whenever it felt like it. It grew in some of the most unlikely places though it certainly didn't grow in our part of South Dakota.

When I started the eighth grade we moved to Pasco, Washington, a strange desert place with hot, dry winds and little else to recommend it. The move itself wasn't too out of the ordinary. We had moved a dozen times by then.

We bought a new house surrounded by nothing but dirt. Dry sandy dirt prone to blow everywhere and sift through any crack and crevice available. We were desperate to get something growing.

One day we kids went with our Aunty Ardis to help clean out a house she was selling. Clean up was pretty boring, but she told us we could haul home any of the plants in the crowded yard we thought would work in our bare yard.

Armed with a shovel and a box, we dug up a few odd shrubs we thought might not object too much to being moved. One of these was a spindly bush my aunt called a Rose of Sharon. We planted it near the driveway, watered it well and forgot about it.

Most of the other plants fell over dead by summer's end. The Rose of Sharon shed its few leaves and stood there sheepishly until spring when it sprouted a few green leaves. That was about all it could muster that season.

The next spring was another story. Leaves and fat buds covered the tree. Soon the buds opened into a mob of purple flowers. It was indeed a resurrection.

Years and years later when we were living on the Illinois farm, I found an ad in a garden catalogue for Rose of Sharon bushes. I ordered one. One turned out to be one bundle. I had two dozen sticks that purported to be Rose of Sharon trees. I planted them along the driveway since that seemed like the proper place for such plants. Everyone of those sticks became a small tree and bloomed like crazy that spring. Some were white or pink, but the majority were purple. More resurrection. Maybe the plants were well named after all.

The Pink Stone

The lady at the small shop at the hotel tried to direct me to the jewelry in the glass case. I ignored her and pointed to the pink rock. 'Please,' I said. 'May I see it?'

We were in Yekaterinburg, Russia for a math meeting. It was deep into September and Yekaterinburg is in the Ural Mountains on the meeting line of East and West.

I had actually brought a jacket with me. A rare occurrence. I had traveled over the mountains from Sweden to Trondheim in early May with only a thin sweatshirt. That same sweatshirt had served me through another September trip in Eastern Europe until I finally had to give in to the cold winds and buy a coat in some Romanian town.

Jewelry was not tops on my 'must have' list. The pink rock was another matter. I had a couple of tiny polished specimens of Rhodonite the size of sugar cubes, the kind that dealers sell five for a dollar at Gem and Mineral shows. This was no kiddie rock. This one was a cut and polished slab the size of my hand. And I wanted it.

Rhodonite is an uncommon mineral found in a few isolated locations around the globe. Yekaterinburg is one of those places. This stone is a pink manganese silicate veined with a matrix of black manganese oxide. This specimen was a perfect balance of pink and black.

The rock smith who polished this stone was a master at keeping the surface even. A feat because of the great difference in the hardness of the pink and the black of the stone. He had even cut the bottom of the rock so it would stand upright.

It was love at first sight.

When the meeting ended, I had paid a visit to the church built over the place of the last Czar's death, the marker of east and west, a modern shopping center with high end shops, and several amazing art museums. The pink stone was wrapped in my spare socks and stowed in my backpack. Our ride to the airport was right on time for our 5 am flight to Helsinki. Another successful journey with a worthy souvenir.

Made in the USA
San Bernardino, CA
24 January 2018